1

Lean Competitive Advantage

Lean Drivers for the New Reality

Lean Competitive Advantage

Lean Drivers for the New Reality

By

Robert Devine Jr.
Ronald L. Buckley

Sax Macy Fromm
Clifton, New Jersey

ISBN-13: 978-1483961804

ISBN-10: 148396180X

Published by
Shady Brook Press
14 Shady Brook Lane
Norwalk, CT 06854

Other Books by Ron Buckley

Winning in a Highly Competitive
Manufacturing Environment
Ronald L. Buckley

No Eraser Needed:
Mistake Proofing Your Business
Ronald L. and Candace-Lynn Buckley

My Toaster's Grandfather:
A Simple Look at Lean Operations from a
Toaster's Point of View—One Slice at a Time
Ronald L. and Lucinda A. Buckley

Winning Manufacturing Solutions:
Optimizing Performance
With Lean Strategies
Ronald and Lucinda Buckley

Highly Effective Lean Teams
Ronald L. and Candace-Lynn Buckley

Mistake Proofing Your Business
Ronald L. and Candace-Lynn Buckley

DEDICATION and ACKNOWLEDGMENT

This book is dedicated to two wonderful men: Allan L. Levey – the consummate visionary for business and industry and Leonard N. Stern – the most complete and honorable business person that I have had the opportunity to learn from and grow with.—(Robert Devine)

We acknowledge the contribution of the marvelous men and women with whom we have had the great privilege of working with over the years. We profoundly hope that this book conveys the tremendous respect and gratitude we have for these people and their efforts.

Contents

Chapter 1

Chapter 1

What Does It Mean to Be Lean?

The great recession of 2008 was the result of several factors: The end of an economic cycle, speculation in real estate, easy access to capital and the transformation of the economy. Much discussion has been made about the first three and not enough about the transformation of the global economy. As the United States and most of the world struggled with little or no growth, companies were forced to look inward to sustain themselves and improve earnings. Much of the reason for such a prolonged period of low growth was the transformation of the economy. The technology revolution has advanced to where just about everything is transparent. This visibility is forcing the marketplace to become much more efficient. Any activity involving labor, material, equipment or process that is not efficient – does not add value to a product or service – *must be eliminated*. This is what many companies have been focusing on since 2008 – the elimination of waste. To date much of the low hanging fruit ripe for the picking in the pursuit of the elimination of waste has been picked. As the economy continues to move sideways and slowly recover, it is more critical than ever for all companies to engage all their resources in becoming Lean and Efficient – *the new reality*.

15

What is Lean? "Lean is a system of process improvement designed to eliminate waste through the application of lean practices and tools optimizing value with the most efficient use of capital, equipment, and materials." Capital includes your people and their talents, equipment includes your business systems, and material includes all the material you use in the process of satisfying your customer's requirements. Lean lowers costs, greatly improves competitive advantage, is applicable to all types of businesses, and creates a cultural transformation in your business.

In today's fast-paced, rapidly changing business environment, companies can no longer just count on the business Leader or even the Leadership Team to manage the business. You must involve all your employees in the success of your company. Your van driver is no longer just a driver. He or she must come to work every day seeking better ways to do his or her job. Every employee must be aware of the processes they use to execute their duties and continually be searching for ways to do their job better—error-free. Continually improve or perish.

Consumers are in the driver's seat: they want the highest quality at the lowest possible cost and they want it when they want it. When *they* want it; not when you promise it, but when they want it. Gone are the days when it was enough just to deliver when you promised. If your promise does not coincide with your customer's desire, he will consider you late even if you deliver when promised. If you can't satisfy your customer, soon someone else will.

Relationships with customers and clients are no longer enough to keep the business. Your customers are under the same pressure you are. They will be forced to seek the price, quality, and service they need regardless of your longstanding relationships. When a better deal comes along, they will be forced to take it. You and your customers will be forced by smaller profits, global competition, and, in some cases, an oversupply of product and services to go elsewhere.

16

Product life and profitability cycles are shortening. Look at the smartphone introduced a few years ago and originally dominated by one player. Now there are several players and a few who could not keep up have already been dismissed. Even the players left standing have to introduce an updated version every few months just to maintain their superior position. Life cycles that use to be five to ten years have been reduced to months in some cases. Digitization has ushered in a new era of hyper-competition.

Intellectual property is under pressure and does not offer the protection it once did. Smaller businesses are at a disadvantage when defending their patents and other forms of intellectual property. Large companies can afford to spend millions on legal fees, whereas smaller companies can't bear the expense of defending their positions. Add to this the shortening lifecycles of products caused by rapid advances in technology and intellectual property protection becomes greatly minimized.

So where does all this leave us? It leaves us in a situation in which it is very difficult for most companies to pass cost increases on to their customers. Customers will simply look elsewhere—they will be forced to consider alternatives due to the above circumstances. They will not be able to just pay and then pass on the cost to their customers. If they are the end user, they will not be willing to pay more for the same value they can get elsewhere. Consumers recognize that there is only so much money to go around in an environment where incomes and net worth have been shrinking. Not to mention concerns about deflation and inflation.

The Need to Create a Very Efficient Money-Making Organization

You must create a very efficient money-making organization to survive. This means you must be able to compete with the best of companies. You do this by becoming a "World Class Organization." By that I mean you must deliver

17

the highest quality services and products at the lowest possible cost when your customer wants them—no sooner and no later. Quality, price and delivery: this is what we all want when we buy goods and services.

To be World Class you must optimize all the productive resources at your disposal. The talent—your employees, the equipment—your business systems employed properly and material that meets or exceeds your customers' requirements. Quality levels approaching Six Sigma (3.4 failures per million opportunities) with an ultimate goal of zero defects in everything you do. Failures and errors virtually eliminated. Cost reduction becomes part of the culture—credits and refunds must be kept near zero. Keeping customer commitments constantly, which includes delivering when the customer wants you to. This is where your business must be.

To do this we have to accept and bring all our employees to accept the following. The key responsibilities of **ALL employees,** not just the Leaders in your business, must be to:

- Generate profits for our stakeholders—if we don't generate profits, how will we stay in business? Everyone involved in the business must clearly understand this. It always amazes me how many people are surprised when I tell them that the primary goal of the for-profit business that employs them is to make money.

- Provide a healthy, happy work environment for the employees. I usually never get an argument with this one.

- Perpetuate the business. This not only encompasses paying your taxes, obeying the laws, getting the proper permits, being a good corporate citizen, etc. It also includes reinventing the business when necessary. For many companies, this is a cultural transformation that

18

involves getting everyone to sign up and participate in making the business the best that it can possibly be. And I do mean every employee and stakeholder, no matter what they do for the business.

The ideas in the pages that follow will clearly show you how to get all stakeholders involved in making your business a very efficient money-making organization.

Motivation, Empowerment and Employee Evaluation

Motivation, empowerment and employee evaluation start with setting expectations. Use the employee evaluation process to set individual expectations by detailing what you expect the employee to accomplish over the next year—job-related goals as well as personal development. There is magic in a quantified objective. If you tell an employee to go off and save me some money on purchase costs, you will get one reaction, and you will get quite another if you tell that employee to go off and save 20 percent or $10,000,000 on purchase costs. In addition to empowering your people through the employee evaluation goal-setting process, empowerment will come through your Lean Drivers.

Why Many Lean Programs Fail?

There can be several causes, a few are addressed here. Unfortunately they all can be traced to a failure of Leadership. Management's failure to get everyone in the organization involved in Lean, including extending the programs to the Management process itself, is a costly error. Lean touches every part of the business. Everything every employee does in their daily work is done with a process. Who is executing these processes? The employee, of course, so then why do so many Managers and so called Lean experts think they have all the answers when it comes to implementing Lean? Well, they don't have the answers no

19

matter how much Lean training they have had. The employees actually executing the processes are the real experts; they know how they are currently executing their processes better than anyone.

This is why we need to target everyone in the organization with Lean education – everyone who executes a process of any kind and that is everyone. Of course, everyone must be educated, trained and inducted into the Lean Program so they have the necessary knowledge and skills required to identify waste, eliminate waste and optimize all resources they are responsible for.

Given the proper skills, employees will be highly motivated to eliminate work problems that cause them grief. They will come up with the solutions – maybe not the exact same solution someone else would come up with, but a solution they will be highly invested in and motivated to implement – it will be their idea. You may not consider their idea as elegant as yours; however, imposing your idea will have a much smaller chance of success just because it was not their idea.

A company is not Lean until all are educated, trained and inducted into the Lean process. This recognizes that management can't do it without the people. A Kaizen here and a Kaizen there just doesn't cut it no matter how much Lean lingo you master. If your Lean program is not structured properly, we find that a few months after the Kaizen, the employees will revert back to their old habits.

Programs that focus on hiring outside experts to come into an organization and direct the Lean effort have a much lower chance of success than programs that focus on educating the entire organization and then letting them figure it out.

We have had several opportunities to follow Lean experts that have failed at a Lean implementation. Following the consulting arm of one of the major accounting firms was

20

particularly difficult. The failed effort had been so painful in everyone's mind that it had turned them against the Lean concept.

If Management is committed to having everyone in the organization involved – coming to work each and every day making the Company better, the transition to Lean will be effective and provide the organization with a competitive advantage. Identifying, prioritizing and implementing solutions for all process issues, starting with the most wasteful and progressing down the list until all issues are fixed and optimized, will become second nature – **Continuous Improvement**. Once all issues identified by the organization are addressed – the process begins again, thereby keeping the organization focused on doing the right thing, eliminating waste and making money each and every day.

Before we move on to the Lean tools themselves, let's look at how to evaluate the overall business so that we know which tools to focus on. The Strategic Planning process can be of great assistance in getting all members of the Leadership Team on the same page. The process usually starts with interviewing key employees to find out how they view the organization. A SWOT analysis to analyze the Strengths, Weaknesses, Opportunities and Threats to the business is developed from the information gathered in the interviews. Other analyses, such as the company's competitive position by product and market, will usually be developed. The Leadership Team then secludes itself to put together a consensus "go forward plan" based on the information previously gathered. Formal one to three-year goals are set, action steps are defined with timelines for each member of the Leadership Team and score cards are created to track performance. An aggressive vision statement is crafted by the Team to define direction for the organization.

If you don't go through with the entire Strategic Planning process before embarking on a Lean campaign, at least execute the interviews of key employees, as well as the

21

SWOT analysis piece. They will certainly point you in the right direction.

Chapter 2

Chapter 2

The Strategic Planning Process

What is Strategic Planning?

The Strategic Planning process participants define where a business is (what is the current state of the business) and next the participants contemplate the opportunity that could exist without any limitation in capital and other resources. The process provides the Leader and the Management Team the opportunity to step out of the day-to-day focus and envision what could be. Strategic Planning, if performed properly can be transformational ... moving the business ahead to become a goal-oriented organization driven to attain its Vision. Strategic Planning is not just for the big guys anymore – all businesses big and small must perform using all aspects of the Strategic Planning process to insure they remain competitive and are able to take advantage of changes in the marketplace. The new economy with its extended period of limited growth is forcing businesses to review all resources – materials, people and equipment – to make sure all activities are adding value to its products and services. The marketplace is moving toward ever increasing efficiency and visibility. All companies must respond by getting in the game or face the reality that they will cease to be competitive and be quickly eliminated.

25

Many companies engage in Strategic Planning as a one off - once a year or once every few years. Strategic Planning is viewed as a necessary evil and is not considered part of the day job. In fact, most businesses do not seriously plan until there is a major problem with their business. Of course, all hands are on deck when there is a problem, all are forced to deal with threatening issues and face trends that they have ignored for years. Please perform the Strategic Planning process when things are going well – use it as a tool to anticipate the market and drive real positive change in the business. Repeat the process annually. Avoid using the process as an annual show-up no prep meeting where the engagement turns out to be a non-fact based anecdotal discussion that insures the business will go nowhere thereby missing opportunities to meet and beat the competition.

Successful businesses have a couple things in common – they have a robust Strategic Planning process that is driven by completing tasks, attaining goals and 100% accountability. The second is a culture of continuous improvement. These tools can only work best if they are imbedded in the core of each organization requiring total openness with visibility – eliminating secrets and personal agendas… the only goal is to work every day to make money for the company! A good and thorough Strategic Plan focuses an organization on activities that deliver results toward achieving the Leader's Vision for success. Success can be defined and measured in many forms – revenue, market share, profitability or a competitive advantage which can be achieved by having lower costs – better products – faster turnaround – lower inventories. Success is whatever it takes to separate a Company from its competitors, make it invaluable to its vendors and desirable for employees and prospective employees! A well run business provides stakeholders with options – an acquisition or merger, develop a new product or service or sell the business, etc.

The bottom line - Strategic Planning is one of the most critical parts of running a business – all must focus on the proper use of resources … capital – people, material and equipment. Gone are the days of running a business through the use of budgets that are based on spending just because that is the way it was done in the past. The market will not allow for expenditures on activities that do not add value to the end product or service. The Strategic Planning process insures all resources are dedicated to measurable and productive tasks necessary for success. A key ingredient for a successful Strategic Plan begins with the CEO or Leader of the Company. He or she must build a consensus plan with the entire Management Team or Leadership Team, no sidebars - no defections. There has to be buy in on all actions, they must be time bound and be assigned to only one person – the person who is ultimately responsible for delivering the targeted result. Also, there must be an incentive plan which is based on pay for meeting the strategic initiatives or **K**ey **P**erformance **I**ndicators (KPIs) of the Strategic Plan. The responsible individual should have access to all necessary company resources to make sure the KPIs and targeted results are met – this individual is the one accountable for delivering that outcome.

Strategic Planning Process Requirements for Success:

Use an outside facilitator, not the CEO or a member of Management. Often Management prefers to handle the Strategic Planning Process on their own – we can do this on our own – let's save the money. Yet, they lose so much. A good facilitator will keep the process on track, be objective and keep the participants from wandering off into the weeds, where they can get bogged down, causing the session to become mediocre and not come close to achieving what is required to move the business forward. An outside facilitator will provide the CEO with an opportunity to sit back and see who has game and who does not. It will be an eye opener for the CEO to observe how his people perform during the session. It will become clear who the most capable contributors are toward achieving the company's vision and who the obstacles are. It will be easier to make personnel decisions after observing how people in responsible positions perform under these circumstances. Remember the Leader is going to drive this process based on the Company's Vision. He or she needs to hear from the participants how they are going to get there. The CEO should always be the last to contribute on each topic to make sure the dialogue is not about making the CEO happy - the dialogue should be about making money for the Company.

The plan should be updated annually. Although you may make a major effort at studying your market strategy and researching your competition every other year, you must update and review your Strategic Plan annually to understand the successes and failures of last year's plan ... and also to agree on what must be accomplished for the new year. It is a good idea to open the session with a 5 to 10 minute report from each participant detailing how they performed against last year's plan. Were their targets met – if not, why not? What was learned and what needs to be done to improve the performance to meet next year's plans.

Get deep into the organization by updating the SWOT Analysis annually. A SWOT analysis is an analysis of the Strengths, Weaknesses, Opportunities and Threats to the business and is developed from the information gathered in interviews with key employees. Conduct one-on-one interviews to determine what works well, what does not work well, what keeps the people in the organization up at night, where the company is on Vision & Strategy, what the interviewee would do if they were the CEO, how does the company execute on product, service and any other measurable metric in the business. Ask for opinions about trends and processes that need attention. The output of this exercise allows the facilitator to narrow the focus – the results of the SWOT analysis are drafted to indicate the frequency of

28

each issue. This helps to eliminate the debate about what is important and what has to be addressed. It is truly amazing that so many companies in different industries have the same issues – accountability, execution and completing tasks on time successfully.

The Strategic Planning process starts with the pre-work which ultimately becomes a driver for the meeting. Taken seriously, the pre-work will prepare the participants for the session by making them think through suggested initiatives and challenges.   Unprepared members waste everyone's time because they are not basing their contribution on facts or data. A pre-work appendix consisting of a collection of industry research from trade associations, internet reports on the competition – companies' both public and private industry sales and mergers and acquisitions help to provide a common background for all of the participants. This information is critical so the meeting is not conducted in a vacuum – missing opportunities, actions by competitors and industry trends.

Prepare a "business as usual" forecast so the Management Team can see clearly the dangers of a business losing momentum and not growing as it should for an extended period of time. Organizations that have a robust planning process are not reacting but, instead, they are driving the business forward.

Review the Company Vision – is it still relevant? Are the Values driving the business to attain the Vision? Many company visions have become politically correct and sound more like Mission Statements than Visions. Often they contain statements such as "we want to partner"… "we want to be the first to be considered," … "we are the best." The Vision must be a call to arms. The competition is focused on taking your business, so you have to make sure you are ready for war – going to market with the purpose of winning. Visions like world domination, number one market share, growth driven by innovation, selling into all channels of distribution, the elimination of or taking business from a competitor

29

galvanizes an organization to make sure every action is focused on meeting the plan and ultimately attaining the Vision. Shame on companies that do not clearly communicate or even understand where they are going … how does the organization know what to do, why they are there and what success looks like? Remember you cannot afford to waste any of the precious resources and they all must be adding value! An engaged and informed workforce can insure that a company will meet the Strategic Plan.

Strategic Initiatives or KPIs are the actions that must be completed on time and within budget to insure that a plan is met. All initiatives have to be measurable activities that drive the business to achieve the Company's Vision. It is important to limit the number of initiatives that drive the Strategic Plan to insure that only the most important actions are resourced and completed. Too many plan initiatives become an organizational excuse leading to failed plans. Make sure the plan is focused and targeted – no excuses. The CEO and Management Team must deliver on all agreed initiatives to set an example for the rest of the organization and demonstrate that performance counts. Ultimately the discipline of a good formal focused Strategic Plan transitions the business to a meritocracy.

Scorecards summarize all strategic initiatives that must be met and rolled up into the Master Scorecard (see examples below). The Master Scorecard is owned by the CEO. The CEO is responsible to manage the business to meet the targets and goals for the overall company. After creating the Master Scorecard the next step is to draft Scorecards for each member of the Management Team. They will include department specific deadlines, KPIs, goals and budgets. The Management Team in turn drives their Scorecard initiatives down through their organizations to their direct reports so they can work to deliver on their specific targets. This process eliminates silos in the organization and focuses everyone in the entire business to deliver on the initiatives that will contribute toward achieving the Company's Vision. The link

30

can be several common targets for example: net income, EBITDA, new product success and cost reductions. The targets are linked through the incentive plan to insure Management works together for the success of the business. The world has changed and all organizations must eliminate excesses and waste. If the Company wins, the employees win, creating a happy and healthy work environment.

The cultural transformation to permanently move an organization from an environment where no one is held accountable to one where everyone is held accountable through a formal plan with KPIs, assignments, targets and due date. The cultural transformation will take at least two years to achieve. Successful businesses manage for results. Nevertheless, after the first year of using a formal Strategic Planning process successfully, many managers will try to push back – not wanting to be held accountable. It is critical for the Leader to stand his or her ground and forge ahead, deciding to stay in a world of focused KPIs with complete accountability. Soon the organization will be able to deliver on its formal Strategic Plan each and every year.

The Strategic Plan is the backbone of the business – the road map to achieve the Leader's Vision by efficiently using all resources available to add value at every step along the path to achieve the Company's desired success. The Strategic Plan is the key that sets the organization up for the transition to a lean culture of continuous improvement. The Strategic Plan must insist that the entire organization be involved and be trained in all the lean initiatives. This Plan should contain initiatives such as eliminating slow moving and obsolete inventory, reducing purchase costs, operating improvements and process improvements. Each initiative in the Strategic Plan should have a specific plan of its own with KPIs and action items owned by one person bound by a time line and monetized. The lean journey cannot be a one off – it has to be part of the formal Strategic Plan and everyone has to be involved, especially the CEO.

31

A Few Examples of Our Strategic Planning Successes:

A National Distributor of Commodities lost focus after the 2008 recession and struggled to regain its market share. By 2013 the company doubled its business by utilizing a robust Strategic Planning process to focus the activities of all department heads on targeted KPIs, budgets and goals. All senior management was held accountable to meet those goals and their incentive plan was tied to overall company results. The last few years have been very positive for the Company and its Management.

A Professional Services Firm had no growth for five years. They had no Vision, no plan just moving along aimlessly. The Managing Director realized that the firm was going nowhere. He had to do something to move the organization forward, so we recommended an aggressive and formal Strategic Planning process that established a new Vision – to become a top 100 firm in their industry in the United States. The firm studied the market and set initiatives to attain the Vision in 5 years – well, the firm will attain that goal in half that time – simply because the entire organization was held accountable to drive the business to achieve their Vision. They got into the game and felt good about becoming a leader in their industry.

A Records Management Firm, bought by a private equity firm, did not know how to operate in a leveraged environment – not even able to speak the language of their financial sponsor owners. The CEO embarked on an aggressive Strategic Planning process that led to the elimination of unproductive management and focused the organization on improving performance. They have met all EBITDA requirements for 3 consecutive years – delighting their new owners.

32

A major Mechanical Engineering Firm used its Strategic Planning process to go lean. As the recession of 2008 dried up the work projects available, the firm had to reexamine its business; forecasts indicated that revenue could drop by two thirds in the next two years. The Strategic Planning processes incorporated the critical lean driver of Mistake Proofing with a goal to reduce expenses through process improvements saving the Company millions of dollars … the bottom line – the company successfully implemented many improvements allowing it to make more money on less than half the sales than it did prior to 2008 in a happier, healthier work environment.

33

Figure 1 Sample Master Scorecard - CEO

ABC CORP.	20XX MASTER SCORECARD - CEO	
The Company must attain all activities indicated below by the agreed due date to insure the 20XX Plan is attained:		
TOPIC	**STRATEGIC INITIATIVE or KPIs**	**DUE DATE**
1. FINANCIAL	1.1 Increase Company EBITDA to 15%	12/31/20XX
PERFORMANCE:	1.2 Lean Initiative - Gross Margin Improvement from 45% to 47%	12/31/20XX
	1.3 Lean Mistake Proofing - Expense Reduction of $420,000 ($35,000 per month)	12/31/20XX
	1.4 Lean Initiative - Improve Inventory Turns from 2.8X to 3.5X	12/31/20XX
	1.5 Accounts Payable increase days paid by 10 days	12/31/20XX
	1.6 Accounts Receivable DSO improve 5 days	12/31/20XX
2. SALES & STRATEGIC		
GROWTH:	2.1 2013 Sales Targets - $42,000,000	12/31/20XX
	2.1.1. East Region Sales Target $17,200,000	12/31/20XX
	2.1.2. Mid - West Region Sales Target $14,800,000	12/31/20XX
	2.1.3. West Region Sales Target $10,000,000	12/31/20XX
	2.2 New Account JKL - Placement Target $250,000	12/31/20XX
	2.3 Account XYZ Plan Sales increase $800,000 - re-launch of brand	12/31/20XX
	2.4 Grow Industrial Sales increase $400,000	12/31/20XX
	2.5 CRM Selection & Implementation - Increase Sales Funnel to 22 Prospects	6/1/20XX
	2.6 Lean - Sales Processes - Revise Returns & Warranties cost savings $100,000	7/1/20XX
3. MARKETING &		
INNOVATION:	3.1 ABC Brand reinvention - new packaging & new placement $1,600,000 revenue	12/31/20XX
	3.2 New Product introduction - 10 products - new revenue of $2,000,000	12/31/20XX
	3.3 Implementation of new advertising campaign - budget $3,000,000	4/1/20XX
	3.4 Market research - update competitor analysis	9/30/20XX
	3.5 Retain 2 outside designers to create new product funnel of 10-20 items	7/1/20XX
4. OPERATIONAL		
EXCELLENCE:	4.1 Lean - Reduction of SLOB Inventory by $1,400,000 reserve for loss $400,000	12/31/20XX
	4.2 Lean - Improve Customer Fill Rate - from 90% to 96%	7/1/20XX
	4.3 Lean - Revise Order Processing consolidate customer service & inside sales	5/1/20XX
	4.4 Lean - Improve On-time Customer Shipments from 85% to 90%	7/31/20XX
	4.5 Lean - Improve New Product Development Process - on time introduction	12/31/20XX
5. HUMAN RESOURCES:		
	5.1 Communicate ABC 20XX Strategic Objectives & Values to Staff - update monthly	2/1/20XX
	5.2 Restructure Organization - Sales - Marketing - Product Development	5/31/20XX
	5.3 Conduct study on IT Software utilization - develop gap training program	7/31/20XX
	5.4 Revise Sales Compensation & Incentive for 20XX - focus on Brand re-launch	2/1/20XX

Figure 2 Sample Incentive Plan

20XX INCENTIVE PAYOUT SCHEDULE			
*Qualifier			
Bonus Target is established at the beginning of the year and will be paid as follows:			
Below 85% of Plan EBITDA	No Bonus Payout		
85% of Plan EBITDA	85% of Bonus Target		
90% of Plan EBITDA	90% of Bonus Target		
95% of Plan EBITDA	95% of Bonus Target		
100% of Plan EBITDA	100% of Bonus Target		
110% of Plan EBITDA	110% of Bonus Target		
115% of Plan EBITDA	115% of Bonus Target		
20XX INCENTIVE VICE PRESIDENT OF SALES POOL $100,000			EBITDA
a. Meet EBITDA TARGET for 20XX			Qualifier
b. Meet Sales Target 20XX			30%
c. Meet Gross Profit Target for 20XX			10%
d. Attain 20XX Accounts Receivable - DSO target			10%
e. Implement Lean Sales Processes savings $100,000			10%
f. Meet Industrial Sales Targets			10%
g. Meet Lean Mistake Proofing Expenses Savings			10%
h. CRM implementation & funnel target			10%
i. Subjective Component			10%

Figure 3 Sample Master Scorecard - Dashboard

TOPIC & STRATEGIC INITIATIVES or KPIs	DUE DATE	PROGRESS REPORT DATE XX/XX/20XX
ABC CORP. 20XX MASTER SCORECARD - DASHBOARD		
1. FINANCIAL PERFROMANCE:		
1.1 Increase Company EBITDA to 15%	12/31/20XX	
1.2 Lean Initiative - Gross Margin Improvement from 45% to 47%	12/31/20XX	
1.3 Lean Mistake Proofing - Expense Reduction of $420,000 ($35,000 per month)	12/31/20XX	
1.4 Lean Initiative - Improve Inventory Turns from 2.8X to 3.5X	12/31/20XX	
1.5 Accounts Payable increase days paid by 10 days	12/31/20XX	
1.6 Accounts Receivable DSO improve 5 days	12/31/20XX	
2. SALES & STRATEGIC GROWTH:		
2.1 2013 Sales Targets - $42,000,000	12/31/20XX	
2.1.1. East Region Sales Target $17,200,000	12/31/20XX	
2.1.2. Mid - West Region Sales Target $14,800,000	12/31/20XX	
2.1.3. West Region Sales Target $10,000,000	12/31/20XX	
2.2 New Account JKL - Placement Target $250,000	12/31/20XX	
2.3 Account XYZ Plan Sales increase $800,000 - re-launch of brand	12/31/20XX	
2.4 Grow Industrial Sales increase $400,000	12/31/20XX	
2.5 CRM Selection & Implementation - Increase Sales Funnel to 22 Prospects	6/1/20XX	
2.6 Lean - Sales Processes - Revise Returns & Warranties cost savings $100,000	7/1/20XX	
3. MARKETING & INNOVATION:		
3.1 ABC Brand reinvention - new packaging & new placement $1,600,000 revenue	12/31/20XX	
3.2 New Product introduction - 10 products - new revenue of $2,000,000	12/31/20XX	
3.3 Implementation of new advertising campaign - budget $3,000,000	4/1/20XX	
3.4 Market research - update competitor analysis	9/30/20XX	
3.5 Retain 2 outside designers to create new product funnel of 10 -20 items	7/1/20XX	
4. OPERATIONAL EXCELLENCE:		
4.1 Lean - Reduction of SLOB Inventory by $1,400,000 reserve for loss $400,000	12/31/20XX	
4.2 Lean - Improve Customer Fill Rate - from 90% to 96%	7/1/20XX	
4.3 Lean - Revise Order Processing consolidate customer service & inside sales	5/1/20XX	
4.4 Lean - Improve On-time Customer Shipments from 85% to 90%	7/31/20XX	
4.5 Lean - Improve New Product Development Process - on time introduction	12/31/20XX	
5. HUMAN RESOURCES:		
5.1 Communicate ABC 20XX Strategic Objectives & Values to Staff - monthly	2/1/20XX	
5.2 Restructure Organization - Sales - Marketing - Product Development	5/31/20XX	
5.3 Conduct study on IT Software utilization - develop gap training program	7/31/20XX	
5.4 Revise Sales Compensation & Incentive for 20XX - focus on Brand re-launch	2/1/20XX	

Chapter 3

Chapter 3

Lean Drivers

Lean drivers are the tools you will use to build your Lean organization. Although many of these tools come straight out of the Six Sigma toolbox, we will avoid getting bogged down with a discussion of a formal Six Sigma program, which many smaller companies would find far too complex and expensive. For those organizations that wish to pursue a full-blown Six Sigma program, there are plenty of resources available. What we are trying to do here is to encourage the use of tools that virtually any company—big or small—can afford and put to good use in short order. The idea is to pay for the cost of the implementation as it is being implemented and then some. A return on your investment should come immediately after you put the tools to work in your business.

The Lean drivers are Mistake Proofing, Self-Directed Cross-Functional Teams, The Workout Process, Flexibility, Succession Planning, and Expense Control. Inherent in all of these tools are the employee motivation and empowerment elements. Any one of these tools can be used separately, but taken together they will enable you to build a very lean money-making business.

Mistake Proofing

Mistake Proofing will enable your employees to identify and fix problem processes in your business so that they will be able to identify when an error has occurred or is about to occur and take action—this is called Lower Level Mistake Proofing. Better yet, it enables employees to prevent the errors entirely through Higher Level Mistake Proofing. It is a way to involve all your employees in building your Lean money-making business. Each and every employee must be trained to identify and Mistake Proof the processes they use in their work. Gone are the days when an employee could be less than a full participant in making your business successful, whatever their job function. The employees who drive your delivery vans are not just your drivers, they represent you and must take their role as a full participant seriously—they are stakeholders in your business!

Self-Directed Cross-Functional Teams

Self-Directed Cross-Functional Teams will be where you address the bigger issues that are not so easily or quickly resolved at the Mistake-Proofing level. They would be used for issues like doubling inventory turns or implementing a company-wide bar-coding system. You will use the resources that currently exist in your business. Select employees from different areas of the business to work together to solve the big problems by meeting challenges given to them by top management. These Teams will work independently without interference from the management that hasn't been able to solve the problem in the past. In fact, this is as good a place as any to say it! I usually ask to address the senior management team before I kick off a Self-Directed Team. Often during that meeting, a member of the management Team starts to tell me how to solve the problem I am about to hand to the Self-Directed Team. My reaction is usually: "WOW, if you had the answer, why didn't you speak up before—you could have made the problem go away before I got here." Of course, he or she did not have the solution and the point is made and the Team goes forward.

The Workout Process

The Workout process is a simple and brilliant way to deal with complex issues in a short period of time, usually two or three days. It is a way to deal successfully with these issues by building a consensus business plan. The output of the Workout is a go forward consensus plan of identified action steps with assigned responsibility and deadlines.

Flexibility

Creating flexibility is essential for success in today's business environment. Cross-training employees to do several different tasks efficiently, as well as having the right materials and equipment when they are needed, is an absolute necessity. The goal here is to create the flexibility you need to react to your customers' changing needs.

Succession Planning

Too often Succession Planning is neglected at your business's peril. This area is essential to the success of any business. Today the world is moving so fast that you have a choice either to stay on top of developing your employees on a continuing basis, or to fire all of them and start over every five years. So, how do you ensure that the organization is continually developing its people? One answer is through the Succession-Planning process. Each key employee must be required to have a plan for his or her succession—at least one person ready and another being prepared. This includes a formal written plan with action steps detailing how each individual is being prepared, forcing each key employee to develop his or her successor. It will build a culture of

41

employee development and will ensure a deep bench—a team player always ready to step in when the opportunity presents itself.

Expense Control

Expense control will contribute greatly to your bottom line and help you set expectations for your people. Remember, you are trying to eliminate all the waste in your business. Watching expenses carefully sends the right message about eliminating waste and everyone can contribute to this effort.

There are, of course, other Lean drivers; however, I chose to concentrate on these because almost any company can easily afford to put these simple drivers to work in their business relatively quickly with a minimum of expense.

Chapter 4

Chapter 4

Mistake Proofing

In this chapter I will use simple language to describe a step-by-step process that can be used to help create a very efficient error-free organization that will be better able to compete with the best of companies. To make a sometimes dull topic interesting, I will draw on my many years of past business experiences and share my real-life challenges in describing situations that everyone can relate to.

I will explore the idea that implementing a Mistake-Proofing program is rewarding, not only as a means to improve profits, but also as a means to achieve great personal satisfaction by developing your employees' knowledge and skills while at the same time providing real job security within their own abilities. Happy employees look forward to coming to work. They not only show up regularly, but they are also continually striving to improve the company's competitive position. Employee development is no longer a luxury that is reserved for corporate giants; it is a necessity for all companies of any size that intend to remain competitive. If a company is going to be successful in the future, it must use and optimize all the productive resources at its disposal. This includes using all the employees' talents in a proactive manner through employee involvement at all levels. In Mistake

45

Proofing your business, employees will get involved in a proactive way if they believe they share in and are part of what is going on in your company. They hunger to be part of the scene and will respond when treated well and like adults who can deal with the realities that affect their jobs.

In the pages that follow I will describe how to move a company into the Mistake-Proofing mode in order to become a very efficient and exciting company, prepared to meet and defeat the competition. It all starts with adjusting management's attitude toward empowering their employees to become full partners in improving every part of the business. I will cover how to establish a training program and lay out in detail the training methods I have used successfully over the years. Included are understanding process errors, the cost of errors, the levels of Mistake Proofing and its tools and methods, as well as some other problem-solving tools.

The process of coming to the realization that change is necessary to a company's survival is frustrating. Others in the organization will still be resistant to change. Management support is essential to the success of any major change in the way an organization functions. Consultants can help and are sometimes necessary, if only to convince others in the organization that management is serious. Great care should be exercised when selecting the right consulting firm to help.

I can't express the delight I experienced with the implementation of these programs. To see employees at all levels, some with less than a high school education, putting together presentations for top management on their own time after hours and then carrying them off in such a sincere and professional manner is a wonderful experience. These employee involvement programs have been the most incredibly beautiful parts of my career. Once you get a taste of this kind of working environment, you need more; it is addictive in the most positive way. What is possible? Just about anything your employees put their minds to is possible.

46

Your people are the best chance your company has to succeed at beating the competition.

There is really nothing very complicated, just simple concepts and ideas that every manager owes to himself or herself and to his or her people: continuous improvement through training and education, open and honest up-front communications and employee involvement.

What we want to do is turn on each and every employee's reticular activating device. Okay, this is as complicated as this process gets—if you want to do complicated you will have to buy another book because you won't find it here. Let's say you want to buy a new car and you drive to a nearby car dealer and test drive a beautiful new Ford Explorer (or another type of car you really like a lot). You start to negotiate with the salesman but leave without the car. On your way home you will see more Ford Explorers than you have ever seen on that road before. Why? Your reticular activating device kicked in. You were sensitized to the sight of Ford Explorers. That's what we want to do to your employees—sensitize them to seeing opportunities in the processes that they use every day to do their work. Just about everything we do we do with a process, but we seldom examine that process to see what we can do to make it a better process. With the right skills we can.

Introduction to Mistake Proofing Your Business (Poka-yoke)

Mistake Proofing was perfected to an art form by the Japanese in their manufacturing processes. I had the great privilege of learning directly from the artist himself, Shigeo Shingo. He came to Yale University at the age of 79 to provide some ideas. He said that he had taken the idea of Henry Ford's production line and the American grocery store from America to Japan, so he was now giving his Mistake-Proofing ideas to America. He called it Poka-yoke—a close direct translation is "fool proofing." The intent is to minimize the

47

possibility of worker error through the use of warnings or to completely eliminate worker errors through "fool-proofing" processes, thus making work virtually error-free. Mistake Proofing is based primarily on simple technology that can be easily grasped by virtually anyone. By applying common-sense solutions that seek to permanently fix everyday problems that arise in the workplace, processes become free of errors, making expensive inspections and checks unnecessary and eliminating costly do-overs and rework. Even 100 percent inspection will not catch all the defects. When mistakes are made repeatedly, look to the process for the solution, not to the operator or person performing the task. Everyone makes mistakes and there are hundreds of reasons for this. Fatigue, boredom, distractions, poor designs, material problems, equipment problems, difficult working conditions, and personal illness are just a few. Very few, if any, workers get up and come to work in the morning with the intention of making as many mistakes as possible that day. Nobody really wants to make mistakes by definition. Once this simple premise is accepted, it makes it easy to look to the processes or designs for solutions to problems. The process design may be a good one that works well; however, perhaps it can be improved by changing the design just a little to make it easier to execute. This is not to say the design is poor, but only that it can be improved.

Today, the advantages of Mistake Proofing have migrated to virtually every area of business. The factory, information technology, accounts payable, accounts receivable, human resources, sales, marketing, distribution and other so-called backroom groups all enjoy the benefits of Mistake Proofing. In addition, I have used these techniques to improve all types of businesses including: manufacturing, construction, health clubs, not-for-profit, accounting firms, records management businesses, engineering firms, retail and distributors, as well as many others. This effort combined with e-business efforts seeks to build a very efficient organization, starting with the process of selling and progressing through the entire business to delivery of products and services. This change has been brought about by the recognition that a process is a process; whether the process is used on the factory floor or in an office environment, it can be enhanced and Mistake Proofed to reduce the possibility of making errors or to eliminate the possibility of making errors altogether.

One of the most powerful characteristics of Mistake Proofing is that everyone in your business can participate. All of us have the natural skill that it takes to be a Mistake-Proofing expert to one degree or another. All that is required is a little training. The training is not expensive and does not require specialized skills to conduct. In fact, the training is more awareness-oriented than anything else. Pick someone in the organization with a reasonable amount of common sense and send him or her off to a seminar to become a trainer on the subject, or kick-start the initiative by bringing in an experienced trainer to train fifteen people or so in a two-day session. You may even choose to do both, or you may hire an experienced trainer and then select an in-house trainer from the first group of fifteen employees you train. You can use this chapter as a guide and develop your own program by closely adopting the precepts herein. Again, pick someone with good common sense who wants the job and is well respected by others in the organization. When the training method has been selected and the trainer is in place, train everyone. The more employees looking for ways to eliminate errors permanently, the quicker the organization will arrive at an error-free environment, or, at the very least, approach an error-free environment.

The training should be formal in that it is scheduled and mandatory, yet it should be kept informal in that everyone should be encouraged to participate in the training activity., Make this a condition of employment, pure and simple. New employees should be scheduled to take the course as part of their orientation. If new employees are hired infrequently, the new employee training can be postponed until enough students are available. However, don't put off training the new employees too long. If new employee contributions are to be

49

maximized, train them early; a fresh set of eyes can see opportunities that have been missed by your current employees. Remember, according to Maurice Nicol, "The longer you are in the presence of a problem the less likely you are to solve it."

Prerequisite: Changing the Way You View Mistakes in Your Organization

Changing the way you view mistakes in your organization is a prerequisite for any Mistake-Proofing program to gain acceptance. Your employees, the ones who actually use and execute the processes you will be Mistake Proofing, must believe and accept that mistakes are not purposefully caused by their co-workers, subordinates, or those higher up in the organization. It must be accepted by all that no one gets up in the morning and says, "I am going to work today to make all the mistakes I can." Certainly, there could be an exception to this rule; however, I have never encountered one in the thousands of employees that I have worked with and I don't ever expect to encounter one. Once you accept this premise, then it is easy to move on to eliminating errors by looking at the process itself or at external influences on the process, such as defective materials, tools, methods, the environment, etc. As long as you focus on placing blame on the individual for mistakes that occur, you will never really eliminate them from your business. Therefore, when you find an error that appears to have been caused by an individual, take a closer look at the process to find the real cause behind the error, and then apply the tools presented in this chapter to prevent the error from ever occurring again.

Examples of Mistake Proofing

As part of the course, each student will be called upon to draw on his or her own life experiences. As mentioned earlier, everyone has had many encounters with examples of Mistake Proofing; some examples are listed below:

- Child-proof locks in the home and car.

- Circuit breakers.

- The light in your refrigerator that automatically goes out when the door is closed.

- Automatic seat belts.

- Smoke alarms that beep when the battery is low.

- Three-pronged plugs.

- Printers that signal low ink levels.

- Automatic lights that come on after dark.

- Electric eyes on doors.

- Grocery store scanners.

- Self-cleaning ovens that lock when cleaning.

- The camera that will not allow a picture to be taken if the lens cover is not removed.

In addition to the common Mistake-Proofing methods we all encounter, many examples can be found in the workplace. Some examples are listed below:

- Double switches on machinery that require both hands to be occupied so that a hand cannot be placed in harm's way when the machine is operating.

- Software that requires an operator check before deleting data.

- Software that requires one to fill in missing data to complete an application.

- Spreadsheets with built-in cross-footing that double-checks the accountant's totals.

51

- Barcode scanners that eliminate keying errors, which are all too common in keyboard entry.

- Relationship databases: these databases compare an actual set of data against a stored, predetermined set of desired data that should be achieved under the given circumstances.

- Photo sensors that detect the presence of an object.

- Automatic on/off timers.

- Notched parts that can only fit one way (three-pronged plug).

- Shaped parts that match the same shape receptacle, allowing only one orientation on contact (USB port and stick).

- Color-coded paper sets that make sure the customer takes the correct copy.

- Test equipment that senses DIP switch settings and will not allow the process to continue until the desired settings are present.

- Circuit board in-circuit testers that exercise the circuit and can check for shorts (opens), component orientation, component presence and component values.

- Scales that check counts.

- Interlocked doors that cannot be opened when another door is open—e.g., in a darkroom where double doors are used to keep out light: when one door is opened, the other door is automatically locked.

- Templates that prevent picking the wrong parts for a specific order or product—the template covers the bins of parts not needed and only allows access to the components required.

•   The serial number comparative database that, similar to a relationship database, does not allow duplicates. Once used, the number is stored in the database and cannot be used again.

Levels of Mistake Proofing

There are two levels of Mistake Proofing. The first level (the lower level) makes it easier to recognize when an error is about to occur or when an error has just occurred. An example of Mistake Proofing that makes it easier to recognize when an error is about to occur is the warning buzzer that warns you that your keys are about to be left in your car's ignition. Another example is word processing software that uses a dialog box to warn that you are about to delete an item or save a new document that will replace an existing document. These are based primarily on warning alert signals. An example of Mistake Proofing that makes it easier to recognize that an error has already occurred is the tray that contains a pin that was supposed to go into the sub-assembly that was just passed on to the next manufacturing stage. If the pin had been used on the previous assembly, the container would be empty when the next setup was prepped. In this case the operator places only the parts required to build one sub-assembly prior to starting the assembly process. If any parts remain in the bins after completing the previous sub-assembly, they will be detected at this, the setup point. It is at this point that it becomes obvious that a part has been left out of the previous assembly. These are the least desirable Mistake-Proofing methods in that an error can still occur. The next level is the most desirable.

The second level (the higher level) of Mistake Proofing, the most desirable, is the prevention of an error from occurring. With these methods the process is designed not to allow an error to occur. The process may shut down if an error is about to occur, or the design of the Mistake Proofing will simply not permit an error to occur. As one progresses from the lower levels to the higher levels of Mistake Proofing, the process is less dependent on the operator for error-free performance. An example of these Mistake-Proofing methods is the final test equipment that does not allow the final test to be completed unless the DIP switches are set exactly as the software just downloaded into the final product dictates. Another is the notched component that only fits one way in the mating item (USB port) or the component that works no matter which way it is inserted. Yet another is a database that will not allow you to enter numbers in an alpha field, assign a serial number that has been previously assigned, or pay a bill with an invoice number that is the same as an invoice number on a bill that has previously been paid for the same account. These types of Mistake-Proofing solutions permanently resolve your mistake-causing issues by not allowing these mistakes to occur in the first place. Often when a higher-level solution is not immediately evident, it makes sense to implement a lower-level solution first that provides a warning that a mistake is about to occur or has occurred, to be followed at a later time by a better, higher-level solution that will not allow the mistake to occur in the first place. An excellent example of this is the test equipment mentioned above that will not allow the test to be completed unless the DIP switches are set correctly. The first real-life iteration of this Mistake-Proofing process simply presented a picture on the display of how the DIP switches would look if they were set correctly, alongside another picture of the way the DIP switches were actually currently set. The theory was that the test operator, seeing how the switches were supposed to be set next to an image of how they were actually set, would fix the problem. In fact, it solved 99 percent of the problems, but we were after a 100 percent fix. The next higher level of Mistake Proofing, preventing the test from being completed unless the switches were set correctly, came later and was the 100 percent fix we were looking for. The important thing to remember is: when you find a lower-level solution, keep looking for the solution that completely eliminates errors by preventing them altogether.

Tools and Methods of Mistake Proofing

The tools and methods of Mistake Proofing are many and varied. The only limits are the extent of the creative abilities and imaginations of the individuals doing the Mistake Proofing. Cost can also be a limiting factor. However, if one method is too costly, find another less costly method that gets you close to a 100 percent solution. Sometimes the method that is chosen may not be the most desirable, yet it may be the only one affordable. Some of the various tools and methods are listed here, though the list is by no means exhaustive:

- Bar-coding that eliminates keying data.

- Motion detectors—checking for movement or presence.

- Contact devices—checking for presence.

- The design—shape of the design.

- Comparative databases—checking for the equivalent or the non-equivalent.

- Software that tests for data with specific characteristics.

- Scales—checking for presence, volume or size.

- Using components as conductors that power equipment.

- Counters—checking quantity for presence.

- Pass-through holes—checking for size.

- Control charts—allow for control of the process.

- Templates—ensure access to correct items.

- Photo cells—checking for presence, size, quantity or quality.

55

- Colors—simple form identification.

The Fun Factor

One of the nicest parts of Mistake Proofing is that it is fun work. No engineering degree is required, only common sense. Everyone can get into the act. The next blockbuster idea can come from anyone. Employees from all levels of the organization and all walks of life get to work together to resolve problems. This will lower costs and improve quality; what a great way to apply an employee's talents and energy.

Mistake Proofing: The Story

The following section is devoted to a selection of real Mistake-Proofing examples. They are actual accounts of Mistake-Proofing opportunities involving some of America's best companies. I hope you, the reader, will find some of the circumstances familiar and will be able to correlate some of the solutions found on these pages with opportunities in your own companies.

Paying the Same Invoice Over and Over

While working in a New Jersey company, I was asked to approve a vendor's invoice. Since the invoice had already been approved by another company Vice President reporting to me who assured me that the services had been provided, I signed, my signature serving merely as a rubber stamp that was needed because the invoice amount exceeded the VP's approval limit.

Well, two weeks later, after receiving an e-mail from an irate Controller asking why I had approved an invoice that had just been paid for the second time, I found myself confronting the VP who originally convinced me to sign the invoice for payment approval. After some research, to the embarrassment of all involved, the VP came to me with proof that the bill had not only been approved and paid twice, it had actually been paid three times. The same invoice for the same services had been submitted three times, approved for payment three times, and paid all three times. Of course, the funds were recovered from the vendor in the form of a credit.

How could the Accounts Payable process that would allow the payment of an invoice three times for the same services to the same vendor be Mistake Proofed? Simply write a program that compares and rejects the payment of any invoice with the same invoice number to the same approved vendor for the same amount and the problem is solved. As it turned out, it was a very easy program for the Information Systems group to write and implement.

The Contest Is Over

A packaging group in a consumer products company had designed a new package for a marketing campaign that included a postcard-sized insert offering the contest winner season tickets to all home games of a popular baseball team. The problem was that the product introduction was delayed by several months after the baseball season had ended. To add insult to injury, the expiration date on the entry form had passed ten years before the forms were printed. The Mistake-Proofing solution: use software that will not allow the creation of dated material after the date selected has passed.

More Packaging Trouble

The packaging design group routinely used the copy and paste function to save time in designing a package that was very similar to an existing package. The problem was that both products ended up with the same item number. Some customers were being shipped the wrong product. The Mistake-Proofing fix: use a comparative database that will not allow the same part number to be assigned more than once. This Proofing method was also used in Connecticut to prevent using the same serial number more than once on more than one piece of medical equipment. It was important that each piece of equipment have a unique number so the item's entire life history could be traced back to the day the serial number was assigned and forward to the day the item was permanently taken out of service.

How Fresh Is That Fresh Food?

The management of a chain of pet supply stores with a self-service section complained that the food items were spoiling in the bins before they were purchased. The problem was that store employees were not cycling the older product out first. The product on the bottom of the bin was being buried by the newer product when the bins were refilled. The Mistake-Proofing solution: install gravity-fed bins that are angled so that they can be filled from the back, allowing the customers access from the front and so ensuring that the oldest product is taken first.

Turning Off the Jacuzzi

Several times during the course of a year, employees supervising kids' birthday parties would find it necessary to turn off the Jacuzzi to encourage youngsters to get out of the pool when the party was over and usually just before the next party was to start. Unfortunately, turning off the Jacuzzi also turned off the pool circulators. When the Jacuzzi was turned on again with the same switch that turned it off, this did not start the pool circulators. This would burn out the pool heaters and upset the pool's chemical balance, making it necessary to cancel activities in the pool to comply with state law until the chemical balance was restored. The pool downtime was far more costly than replacing the pool heaters.

The first Mistake-Proofing solution the Team came up with was to train everyone working birthday parties at the pool to start the circulators after they shut down the Jacuzzi. This was a LOWER-LEVEL solution. After further discussion, the Team came up with an UPPER-LEVEL solution: separate the

58

circuitry so that turning off the Jacuzzi does not affect the pool circulators.

Note: some of these solutions seem obvious after they surface and one could ask why it wasn't obvious earlier. The answer is that we routinely just step over problems, not recognizing that they are fixable: we were not sensitized to identifying and finding solutions to process issues—our Reticular Activating Device was not turned on.

Power Losses Cause Tennis Bubbles to Collapse

When the utility power was lost and the backup generators did not start after normal business hours, the tennis bubbles that require power to maintain positive pressure would collapse, tearing away from attached buildings and crushing lighting fixtures. Although this was rare, it was very costly when it did occur.

The Mistake-Proofing solution: have the alarm company notify employees in the middle of the night when power is lost and the generators do not start. The alarm company has three numbers to call, one after another, until they reach someone close by who can go in and get the generators going before damage is done. This service was added to the service already in place with the alarm company for no extra cost.

Late Starts and Early Quits in the Construction Business

At a construction company in the Southwest, one of the biggest problems was workers showing up late and leaving early from construction sites. All of these employees had bar-coded IDs. My first choice for Mistake Proofing this problem would have been to scan the employees in and out, and then only pay them for time worked. However, this was not what

59

the workers wanted to do and the best solution is usually the one that the employees want to implement—they will make it work, if it is their idea. Workers were required to sign two forms during the workday relating to work safety and injury. Their Mistake-Proofing solution was to require the employees to sign one of the forms at the gang box before work began and the other at the end of the day. They had to be present to sign the forms. This solution may not have been as elegant as the bar-coding solution; however, it got the company to the same place with a solution that was the employees' idea, not one that was imposed on them.

Construction Foremen Ordering the Wrong Materials

Foremen were ordering the wrong material from the ordering catalog and sometimes two foremen would order the same item.

The Mistake-Proofing solution was to use pictures with bar-codes next to them so that they could be ordered by scanning the item in the picture that matched the description. In addition, the data could be collected easily and duplicate open orders could be detected immediately.

Material Thrown Away on Construction Job Sites

This construction company had decided several years previously that it was less expensive to throw leftover material away than bring it back to the yard, sort it, and then store it. This may have been a good decision when it was made, but the employees knew better. As material cost increased and contracts got bigger, the circumstances changed significantly.

The Mistake-Proofing Team did an analysis, and it became clear that it would be very profitable to hire someone to sort and restock the material, thereby saving the company many thousands of dollars per year.

Time Wasted at a Records Storage Company

Employees charged with the responsibility of retrieving files from records storage boxes in a warehouse containing several million boxes of records did not always have enough ladders or flashlights available. There were always plenty of ladders on the first floor but they were a scarce item on the fourth and fifth floors. In addition, there were several areas of the warehouses that were poorly lit, not necessarily because of poor lighting, but because of the way some boxes impeded the light and made it difficult to find a specific file inside a specific box. Time lost retrieving ladders and time lost going to the office to get a flashlight was a waste of many labor hours.

The Mistake-Proofing solution was to acquire thirty more ladders and to supply each employee with his or her own flashlight. *Simple, yet effective solutions seem obvious after the fact. However, these things often go on for years without ever coming up as an issue. They remain issues we just step over. The Mistake-Proofing venue is so important in assisting management to uncover issues like these.*

Infrared Shorts

One of my favorite Mistake-Proofing methods was used by a manufacturer of LEDs and infrared products in Germany. What a surprise I received when, on a visit to this facility, I suggested that perhaps these products were causing some shorts in our products back in the States. This theory of mine was dispelled quickly once the owner showed me his manufacturing process. The current that ran his equipment was conducted through the components he manufactured for my company. If the components had a short (open), the equipment would stop because the power would stop once the component with the short reached the final stage in the process for each component where it was conducting the power to run the equipment. Voilà, no more components with shorts ever reached this manufacturer's customers.

61

Statistical Process Control (SPC) Leads to Improving Equipment

Imagine a factory floor in Connecticut with thirty shop floor inspectors just hoping to justify their existence by catching an operator making a mistake. Add to this dozens of processes that could not possibly make a good repeatable product. Then mix in a labor union grievance process run amok and you come up with a very nasty, grievance-filled, miserable working environment crying out for a successful Mistake-Proofing program.

One area for improvement in this factory was found in the cable assembly area. During the introduction of Statistical Process Control (SPC), capability studies were conducted to determine each piece of equipment's ability to manufacture a good quality product on a repeatable basis. Almost every connector-staking machine was found to be unreliable. There was a problem with either the tooling, the chosen connector for the wire, or the calibration of the machine. Cables are not sexy devices and engineers do not tend to labor over their design; hence, it is an area ripe for finding low-hanging fruit.

The tooling was repaired or replaced. The correct machine was selected for the correct process and SPC charts were created to monitor the process continually. Reliability and cost were both greatly improved. Prior to this effort, problems were not found until the unit failed final test. This is the most costly place inside your factory to find defects. Units would fail the test (some units went through two hours of testing before failing) and at that point a technician would be required to troubleshoot and repair the unit.

The success of this endeavor, along with similar efforts, increased First-Pass Yield—measured by the number of units that passed test the first time without any rework—from 42 percent to over 99 percent. Although SPC is a great tool in your Mistake Proofing toolbox, it is not the highest form of Mistake Proofing. Using Statistical Process Control minimizes the possibility of mistakes occurring, but it does not completely eliminate the possibility of mistakes happening altogether. Consequently, use SPC as your first line of defense and continue to look for a higher level Mistake-Proofing solution that will completely eliminate the possibility of an error from occurring. One method would be to redesign your product to eliminate the cables through the use of connectors or consolidation of circuits.

By the way, over the next year all thirty inspector positions were eliminated and they were replaced through the Mistake-Proofing process. Many of the inspectors accepted positions as operators. The ones who wanted to remain inspectors left our employment to haunt other area factories. Not a single grievance was filed in this same factory for years after the last inspector left.

Sequencing Processes to Eliminate Building in Batches

The simple task of examining and reorganizing the location of equipment in your facility can lead to Mistake-Proofing solutions while at the same time increasing efficiency. In one factory that manufactured sensors, the simple act of diagramming the flow of the product through the facility revealed a ridiculously circuitous route for one product series. The equipment had been used to manufacture a type of sensor that had become obsolete and was no longer manufactured. However, it never occurred to anybody to combine all the equipment for the new sensor in one area to eliminate queue time, travel time, and batch building. The equipment was moved into one cell, reducing inventory and improving velocity and quality. If a process goes out of control, building in batches lends itself to accumulating multiple defects that go undiscovered until the item is put to use in the next stage of assembly. When a part is immediately put to use in the next stage of assembly, an error that is detectable at this stage is detected quickly before many more defective parts are manufactured. The defect-creating process can be

63

corrected quickly, preventing the creation of further defects. Again, continue to look for a higher-level Mistake-Proofing solution that will completely eliminate the possibility of an error occurring. Your manufacturing cells should always be under review for improvement.

Film Processing

A group of Manufacturing Engineering folks were consolidating and improving a film-winding business in Connecticut from one location in Germany and another in California. This was a medical imaging film product used in the cardio-vascular arena. The short version is this: we purchased very large rolls of film in large quantities and converted them into very small rolls of film (the winding operation), then packaged the film for customers to use in a hospital environment, shipping the film with the appropriate developer. The work had to be done in total darkness, no light whatsoever, and in a cool, dry environment. There were five winding rooms in California and one in Germany. After the move to Connecticut, the entire operation was accomplished in one efficient Mistake-Proofed winding room as described below.

• A revolving door that did not allow any light to enter permitted the operators to come and go without having to shut the operation down. Previously the individual rooms had to be shut down and the product sealed away to protect it from the light when the door was opened to permit entry or exit for any reason. Whenever an operator failed to seal a roll of very expensive film from exposure to light, the expensive film had to be scrapped.

• Another form of Mistake Proofing was accomplished by installing interlocking feeding doors to allow raw film to be fed into the room on one side and the finished product to be passed out of the room on the other side, again permitting continuous operation when moving material into and out of the room. The interlocking mechanism prevented doors from being opened at the same time, thus eliminating the possibility of damaging light entering.

•   In addition, automatic cutters were installed on the rolling equipment, making this operation easy to perform in total darkness and eliminating the possibility of human error.

There were other innovative changes that made the winding tasks easier to perform in the dark. The people involved with this transition had a lot of fun with this very successful Mistake-Proofing project. Long after the room was up and running in full production, they continued to make innovative Mistake-Proofing improvements with equipment and methods.

Eliminating Handling

Eliminating handling steps in the manufacturing process eliminates opportunities for errors at each of the eliminated steps. One example took place in the sensor-manufacturing cell in a Connecticut factory where changing the type of epoxy used in the manufacturing process led to significant improvements. Epoxies that are cured with an ultraviolet light replaced time-and temperature-cured epoxies that had to stand overnight to cure. UV-cured epoxy allows the operator to cure the epoxy immediately after application with a handheld ultraviolet light. The assembly process can continue without the need to rack, stack and wait for the assembly to cure. This eliminates many touches as well as removing the curing queue time from the manufacturing cycle time. In addition, the new epoxies could be purchased premixed from the manufacturer. Buying them premixed eliminated variability in the in-house mixing operation. You can buy many types of epoxies premixed, packed in dry ice and shipped overnight. Usually this is an insignificant part of your product cost and the increased cost of premixed material is usually well worth the elimination of the variations in the mixing process. It also eliminates a job that almost nobody likes.

Oil Leaks

One great example of a problem addressed by a final assembly Mistake-Proofing Team was x-ray housing oil leaks. The rotating anode device that produced the x-ray was sealed in a glass envelope. This tube, as it was called, was assembled into a leaded metal housing that was then filled with oil for cooling purposes. The metal sections had o-ring grooves machined in them and the o-ring seals prevented the oil from leaking out. After the tubes were assembled, they would be tested with high power levels. This test produced a considerable amount of heat. It was at this stage that the oil leaks were detected. These oil leak problems persisted for years despite a great deal of attention from Manufacturing, Engineering, and Quality Control personnel. Machined surfaces were improved, o-ring materials were changed, o-rings were soaked in oil for days prior to being used, and rigid specifications were imposed, but most of the oil leaks persisted. The oil leaks persisted until the Final Assembly Department Mistake-Proofing Team took on the problem.

The Team reviewed the problems carefully using the problem-solving techniques they had learned in the classroom and on the shop floor. Before long they had solved this serious problem. The solution had eluded our best engineers. In the process of assembling the metal-to-metal sections with the o-ring in between, the operator applied petroleum jelly to the o-ring before placing it in the o-ring groove. The assembly specification did not specify how much petroleum jelly to use; therefore, some operators used more than others. Some operators, believing that more is better, applied gobs of petroleum jelly. When the housing was heated during a test, the petroleum jelly turned to a liquid and gave the appearance of an oil leak. Since the oil used in the housing was virtually identical in appearance to petroleum jelly in a liquid state, the housing was deemed to be a "leaker" and the unit was disassembled and reworked at great expense.

66

The Pilot Team figured out what was happening. After all, they were the people closest to the operation, so it followed that with the proper training and motivation they should be the ones best qualified to resolve the problem. In this case, as in so many cases, the problem was not what it appeared to be; the housing was not leaking oil from inside. The immediate Mistake-Proofing solution was simply to correct the work instructions by specifying a light coating of petroleum jelly. The results turned in by the Team in solving this oil leak problem amounted to an 85 percent reduction in oil leaks and more than paid for the entire Mistake-Proofing training program for years to come.

Transaction Simplification

There were plenty of opportunities to simplify the business transactions of transferring inventory from our vendor's inventory to ours. This was done electronically, using a bar-code reader to set up automatically the Accounts Receivable for the vendor and the Accounts Payable for us when material ownership was automatically transferred to our possession. The material was then transacted out of our inventory when the finished item was transacted to final stock with a bar-code wand using the "backflushing" method based on our bills-of-materials. Our system knew which and how many parts were used to build a finished product; it was a simple process to have our business system deduct all these parts whenever we transacted a finished product to the finished goods stockroom from production. With this system, most of our material movement transactions were done electronically, eliminating the hundreds of errors normally created when thousands of items were keyed into the system by hand. Purchase Orders were not necessary; a simple letter of agreement with the vendor covered each item. However, if you find it necessary to use Purchase Orders, they can be created automatically with the signal to fill a requirement or as the requirement is being filled. At the same time, the Accounts Receivable for the Vendor and the Accounts Payable for your company can be set up. The Purchase Order can be opened and closed simultaneously when the requirement is filled. This also works well for consignment inventory.

Eliminating Setups with Dedicated Equipment

In this case the addition of an ultrasonic welder to a work cell eliminated the need for an operator to carry work across the factory to an ultrasonic welder in another work cell, which required a change in setup and the waste of material in adjusting for the new setup. Again, the elimination of the need to manufacture in batches and make the parts as they were needed enabled quick detection of errors so they could be corrected immediately, rather than after a large batch of defective parts had been queued up for production. With the welder right in the cell where the assemblies were consumed, there was no need to change the equipment setup. The parts quality was consistently good, and with preventative maintenance, it remained good.

Customers Ordering Their Own Products Using the Internet

Mistake Proofing was the result of an e-business campaign in Milwaukee. The decision was made to take product information to the next stage and allow customers to place product orders over the Internet, eliminating errors caused by internal order-takers misinterpreting the customer's requirements. Customers were able to order simple products straight from the system or configure complex products on-line. In the latter instance, this saved Sales staff many hours of face time working out order details with the customers. If the sale was for a complex product with many different options and some options were not available on certain models, the automated ordering system was programmed to avoid any ordering errors matching features with models that a salesman might make. Customers were even willing to work out delivery and installation times based on an availability schedule posted and automatically updated on the net. Many customers actually preferred to do their own ordering over the net,

68

especially for more complex products, even though they were fulfilling the role normally filled by the Salesman. They built their own product at their leisure without the pressure of a Salesman's pitch. In addition, customers who used the products and the supplies that went with them found it convenient to order the supplies themselves. This is especially true when they know exactly what they want and are ordering the same items over and over on a regular basis.

Original Equipment Manufacturer Monitors Your Equipment for Optimum Performance

Another fascinating use of the Internet as a tool is its application in diagnostics. In this instance, customers dialed into an equipment service center, hooked up a problematic piece of equipment, and a service technician diagnosed and fixed the problem live in minutes. On one occasion, one of our technicians was able to enhance the resolution of an image. This enhancement was credited with helping doctors save the life of a child. The service was offered with new products to attract new business and was also sold separately with a service contract, which generated another revenue stream.

Large equipment manufacturers are marketing this service as another source of revenue, charging a fee for improving their customer's efficiency. The equipment can be monitored twenty-four hours a day and adjustments can be made while the equipment is running. These techniques are being applied to locomotives and jet engines. Imagine being able to monitor and tweak remotely the equipment you build and supply so that it always performs error-free. Just being able to determine when a customer's piece of equipment needs to be serviced to keep performing at an optimum level, thus delivering error-free results, can bring in a fortune in revenue. What a great Mistake-Proofing opportunity!

69

Component Manufacturer's Database Interacts with Your Design Software

Our Design Engineers had access over the Internet to a vendor's database that helped to determine the most effective electronic component to use in a circuit. The component's functional characteristics, as well as its footprint, could be quickly ascertained using the supplier's database. Some design systems can incorporate this data automatically, preventing design errors from occurring. One nice feature about these vendor sites is that many of them are available twenty-four hours a day, seven days a week. An engineer working on a design at 9:00 pm does not have to wait until 8:00 am the next day to sort out his technical issues with the supplier.

Pick and Pack

A consumer products company shipping to thousands of stores in the USA was picking and packing orders in a huge 500,000 square-foot warehouse. Each order could call for any of 1,500 different items. One group of operators would pick the items, counting the ordered quantities out of bins containing the various products and placing the items in corrugated containers. Another group of checkers would remove the items packed and repack them to be sure the correct items and the correct quantities were present to fill the order. Double work to ensure the customers got what they ordered—the result of several customer complaints. The solution: insert a scale on the conveyor carrying the packaged items to the sealing station. The scale would weigh each carton and the actual weight would be compared with the calculated weight. The calculated weight would be the sum of all the items in the order passing over the scale, traveling in sequence down the conveyor. All the items' weights were known to the business system and the total weight could be easily calculated. If by chance, an order's actual weight and the calculated weight differed, the carton would be moved off to a checking station where it could be checked and corrected. Thus, there was a need to check only a few orders rather than every order. Quite a labor savings, considering the thousands of orders that were processed in this warehouse.

Packaging Equipment

A company which cooked and packaged a product could potentially transfer the dreaded salmonella bacteria from the raw product to the cooked product, thereby contaminating the finished item and necessitating its destruction and costly facility shutdowns for sterilizations. The solution was to split the factory in half, separating each half with a doorless wall. No employee was permitted from one side to the other without proper sterilization. An oven that cooked the product was placed in the wall between the two sides of the facility. The product traveled in the oven from one side of the building to the other. Timers were used to ensure the product was thoroughly cooked and safe from salmonella bacteria before being taken out of the oven for packaging.

Over-Cooked Membranes

Very expensive membranes used in a manufacturing process were boiled as part of the manufacturing process. As luck would have it, one Friday afternoon someone forgot to shut down the equipment that did the boiling. The result: a nasty Monday morning surprise requiring a lot of rework—not exactly the way to start off one's work week. The solution: install timers to shut down the boiling process automatically. This solution was much safer than a pledge never to forget again.

Mother and Baby

Picture a busy doctor with mothers on the maternity floor and newborns in the nursery and neonatal intensive care unit. The doctor needs up-to-the-minute information about a mother and her baby when he is in radiology on another floor,

71

in his office across town, or in his dining room at home. He is reluctant to rely on someone else's interpretations of the up-to-the-minute patient data for mother and baby, which consists of the vital signs, blood test results and images he needs to make his urgent treatment decision. The solution: an information technology system that allows the doctor to access the needed information from virtually anywhere on any device (computer, PDA, smartphone, etc.) connected to the net, thus eliminating the possibility of mistakes occurring in a third party's interpretation, summary, and verbal relay of the patient data.

The above examples clearly demonstrate that Mistake-Proofing opportunities and solutions come in all varieties and sizes. They can dramatically affect both the quality of our output and the quality of our lives in the workplace and beyond. In most cases the Mistake-Proofing solutions are simple. A few of the solutions are more complex to execute, but the technology is there waiting to be applied. The important task is to recognize that the technology needs to be brought together with the Mistake-Proofing opportunity. Next we will move on to using problem-solving tools to help develop robust Mistake-Proofing solutions.

Problem-Solving Tools and Techniques

Problem-solving tools and techniques are an important part of any Mistake-Proofing program. As you will have a variety of talent involved in your Mistake-Proofing activities, keep the tools and techniques in your training simple and easy to understand.

Cause and Effect Diagram

The cause and effect diagram (sometimes called the fish bone diagram) is very effective yet easy to understand. An example is below:

Cause and Effect Diagram (Fishbone)

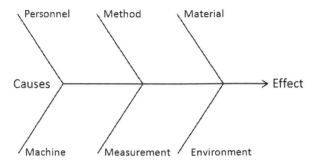

The effect is placed at the head of the arrow and all the possible causes are listed on the legs of the diagram. Each possible cause is then analyzed to determine its contribution to the effect. This technique is easy to use and easy to understand.

Failure Mode and Effects Analysis

This tool is also simple to use and understand. It only takes a little practice to become fond of the Failure Mode and Effects Analysis tool. See the example below:

FMEA

Failure Mode and Effects Analysis

Problem	Consequence	Frequency	Severity	Detection	Score
Wrong amount	Short pay	1	8	2	**16**
Wrong date	Pay late	2	5	5	50
Wrong address	Never pay	4	10	10	400

List the problem in the first column. On the first line in this example, the problem is invoicing for the wrong amount. Consequence—the consequence of invoicing for the wrong amount is being paid short. Frequency—on a scale of 1 to 10, 1 being the lowest, the frequency of this occurring is ranked as a 1. In other words there is a 1 in 10 chance of invoicing for the wrong amount and then being paid short. Severity—on a scale of 1 to 10, 1 being the lowest, the severity of being paid short is 8. In this case you could never be paid all your money, so the condition gets a rank of 8. Detection—on a scale of 1 to 10, 1 being the lowest, the difficulty of detecting the invoicing problem is ranked as a 2. There is a 20 percent chance that the invoice problem would be detected, therefore, it receives a rank of 2, 2 being 20 percent of 10. To determine the score, simply multiply the Frequency times the Severity times the Detection and enter the result in the score column. In this case $1 \times 8 \times 2 = 16$. Repeat this for the other problems identified and list the results in order by score. Address the problems that get the highest score first. You may choose not to address problems that receive a very low score.

Certain characteristics would cause a problem to receive a low score. A very low rank, such as 1, for Frequency, Severity, or Detection would result in a pretty low overall score. For instance: a rank of 4 for Frequency, 10 for Severity and 1 for Detection would result in a total score of only 40. $4 \times 10 \times 1 = 40$. In this example, the problem is highly detectable so the consequences can be mitigated by Detection; hence, a low score of 40. You will want to fix the problem in time, but it will probably not be your most pressing problem needing immediate attention. On the other hand, if Detection had received a rank of 10—meaning that the problem is not detectable, the total score would have been 400. $4 \times 10 \times 10 = 400$. The much higher score of 400 requires immediate action. A high difficulty of Detection rank of 10 gives us a hint that part of a mitigating solution may be to come up with a method of detecting the problem before it can cause a severe problem.

This is an excellent tool to add to anyone's problem-solving toolbox. It is easily explained and understood. Someone who has had little exposure to these types of tools may find using this technique a bit formidable at first. However, after the tool is used just a few times, almost anyone can become comfortable with Failure Mode and

Effects Analysis, making it easy to identify and prioritize the most significant problems that could arise without the emotion that can often send you off in the wrong direction.

Brainstorming

Brainstorming is an excellent method of coming up with solutions to problems. To get my point across, I have often said that I have never met an individual who is smarter than ten dumb people in a room and I know a lot of very smart people. You may think this statement is a bit too dramatic; however, I would ask you to think about it before you jump to that conclusion. There is something magical that happens when you get a group of people together to brainstorm. In a brainstorming session, someone throws out an idea. That idea spurs someone else in the group to get an idea that he or she never would have come up with, had he or she not heard the idea previously thrown out. Multiply this times ten people and the sum is truly greater than the whole. This is the power of brainstorming.

In a brainstorming session, a group of folks sit around a table and brainstorm for ideas. As the ideas are brought up, they are recorded. Some groups use flip charts, other groups use file cards or record the ideas on a PC that is projected on a screen. I like to use flip charts for recording the ideas so that they can be taped to the walls for all participants to reference as the session progresses.

It is important that all ideas be respected, especially unpopular ideas—often the minority ideas bring with them the most effective solutions. After all, if the solutions were so obvious, why would the group need to hold a brainstorming session? The brainstorming should continue until either no more ideas are forthcoming or the ideas that are forthcoming are really dumb ones. At this point the brainstorming portion of the work is called complete by the brainstorming leader and hopefully the best solution to the problem is apparent.

As it is likely that several different solutions emerge to the same problem, categorize them in a four-blocker like the one below.

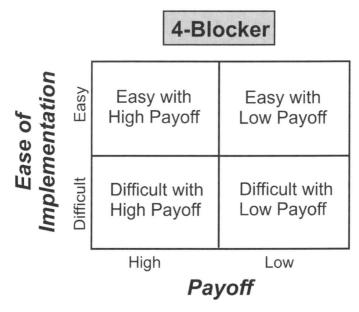

Ideas that are easy to execute with a high payoff go in the upper left quadrant. Ideas that are easy to implement but have a low payoff go in the upper right quadrant. Ideas that are difficult to implement with a high payoff go in the lower left quadrant. Finally, ideas that are difficult to execute with a low payoff go in the bottom right quadrant.

Next, pick the idea or combination of ideas that will give you the highest-level solution to your Mistake-Proofing problem and will be the least difficult to implement.

Six Sigma

Both Statistical Process Control (SPC) and Mistake Proofing (Poka-yoke) are Six Sigma tools, as are Failure Mode Effects Analysis (FMEA) and the other problem-solving tools. We have talked about each of these tools. Of course, each of these tools can be used separately and does not have to be part of a Six Sigma program. Many smaller organizations will shy away from a full-blown Six Sigma program, which can be expensive and difficult to implement. Six Sigma requires a much more complex infrastructure for training and a much larger resource commitment for support than does a Mistake-Proofing program. Sure, it would be nice if the resources were available for a full-blown Six Sigma program; however, much progress can be made using the simpler tools such as Mistake Proofing. So, if you are a smaller organization, start with a Mistake-Proofing program. When you collect from the payoff of your efforts here, move on to Six Sigma, but don't think for a minute that you cannot compete without it.

I would like to make one point here. A Six Sigma quality level would be 3.4 failures per million opportunities while Shigeo Shingo's Poka-yoke methods say do not rest until there are zero defects. Which plane do you want to fly on?

"We Have No Data, But We Are Sure" in Connecticut

Just because we do not have a full-blown Six Sigma program in place does not mean that we do not use Six Sigma methodology to bring some level of structure to solving our problems.

I offer the following in support of the above statement:

I was asked by a friend to assist in one of his companies. The problem was a complete product failure that led to a total product recall and total shutdown of the manufacturing facility. On my first visit I convened a meeting, bringing together about twenty of this company's best and brightest. Virtually all were degreed Engineers and several had advanced degrees, including some with their PhDs. I was told that they were sure they knew what the problem was. The culprit was a sharp metal shard that was piercing a membrane, causing the equipment to short out and fail completely. At that point I said to myself, "Self, you will have

77

this one licked and be out of here in less than five days," and of course I would be a hero with my friend. Well, things didn't quite go the way I thought they would at that moment. When I asked to see the data I was told that they had no data, but they knew the problem was metal shards. I then asked the Team to collect the data. I was told that this would take several days. We called the meeting and agreed to reconvene several days later when the field returns had been inspected and the data had been collected.

The Team reconvened several days later. At that time I was told that we did not have all the data yet; however, now they were sure that sharp metal shards were less than 50 percent of the problem. I knew then that I would be with this company for a while and that my daydream of delighting my friend with a speedy solution was lost. In fact, I spent the better part of ten months with this company. In the end, sharp metal shards did not cause any of the failures. The real cause of the problem was torque pressure.

The approach that brought this company back from the brink was simply to apply Six Sigma methodology in the broadest sense. I insisted that the Team follow the DMAIC method. Define, Measure, Analyze, Improve and Control. Define the problem—in the shard case, defining the problem correctly would have gone a long way toward solving the problem, leading to a Mistake-Proofed solution. Measure—collect and measure the data. Analyze—analyze the data collected. Improve—improve the process/product. Control—put controls in place to ensure that the solution continues to be effective. The result was to bring structure to the company's problem-solving approach.

The problem was identified, fixed and Mistake-Proofed. The Company resumed manufacturing and successfully replaced all customer products that had failed.

These are only a few of the many problem-solving tools and techniques that can be used in the Mistake-Proofing process. These were selected because they are particularly helpful and they are also easy for the trainer to explain and easy for the trainee to understand. I encourage the Team to explore the use of other problem-solving tools and techniques. Meanwhile these will serve to get your program underway.

Laying Out the Program

So you have decided to go forward with your Mistake-Proofing program and you would like to know what the whole program might look like. Well, some possibilities are laid out below.

Select a Program Champion

The individual you select as the program Champion will lead both phases of the training effort. The first phase will entail training virtually all employees, while the second phase will be the ongoing training of all new employees. The Champion should be an individual with some training experience who is well respected by everyone at all levels of the organization. Also, it would be desirable to select a Champion with an understanding of process improvement and the application of problem-solving techniques. Some Six Sigma training would be ideal, but is not necessary.

Kickoff

Make a splash and have some fun with this one. Party, posters and publicity are the order of the day. Whatever you do, get the message across that top management supports this program. Also send the message that everyone will be involved—every employee will be involved. If you are using a Self-Directed Team, they should lay out the program and be part of the kickoff.

The Training

The training includes the following sections:

•   Introduction—Mistake Proofing is awareness training that employs common-sense solutions to eliminate process errors through the use of warnings or by designing processes that completely eliminate the possibility of making a mistake.

•   Defects & Costs. Zero mistakes make for happy customers and happy customers make for prosperous businesses. Prosperous businesses make for more secure jobs. More secure jobs make for happy employees. Fewer errors lead to lower costs and a better competitive advantage. The further into the process it is before you discover a mistake, the more costly it is to fix.

•   Understanding Process Errors. Mistakes are preventable. Look to the process to resolve mistakes, not to the employee. If you have repeated mistakes, chances are there is something wrong with the process, not with the employee. Anyone properly trained should be able to execute a task well. Inspection will not catch all the mistakes.

•   Two Levels of Mistake Proofing (Poka-yoke). Lower-Level Mistake Proofing will warn you that a mistake has just occurred or is about to occur. Higher-Level Mistake Proofing creates a process that makes it virtually impossible to make a mistake with the process. A simple example is the four-drawer file cabinet. At first there was no Mistake Proofing and you could open more than one drawer at a time. If you opened two drawers at once there was a good chance that the file cabinet would fall forward, possibly causing injury. The first attempt at Mistake Proofing was to put a warning message on the front of the file drawers to warn users not to open more than one drawer at a time. This was Lower-Level Mistake Proofing. Nothing prevented you from ignoring the message. The next attempt was to lock all the other drawers once a single drawer was opened, thus insuring that you couldn't open more than one drawer at a time. This was Higher-Level Mistake Proofing—the lock absolutely prevented a second drawer from being opened.

80

- Tools and Methods of Mistake Proofing. They are many and varied and depend only on the imagination of the individual. A few examples are: the shape of items, scales, vision systems, counting method, colors, check lists, instructions, bar-coding, comparative databases.

- Problem-Solving Tools. The Define, Measure, Analyze, Improve and Control tool; Failure Mode and Effects Analysis; Brainstorming; Cause and Effect Diagram.

The training encourages participant interaction in the following ways:

- Counting specific letters in a paragraph to prove that 100 percent inspection is ineffective.

- Requesting that the participants come up with a list for each of the following:

    - Why do they think people make mistakes? Examples are poor designs, fatigue, misunderstanding, personal illness, poor methods, boredom, lack of training, distraction.

    - Common examples of Mistake Proofing. Child-proof locks in the home and car, circuit breakers, the light in your refrigerator that automatically goes out when the door is closed, automatic seat belts, smoke alarms that beep when the battery is low, three-pronged plugs, printers that signal low ink levels, automatic lights that come on after dark, electric eyes on doors.

    - Examples of Mistake Proofing at work. These would depend on the type of business you are in.

    - The kind of errors that could occur in their area of work. *This is probably the most important part of the session.* This is where the participants will identify the things that irritate them in their day-to-day activities. The mistakes that happen over and over and never seem to go away. The ones that are stepped over. Many of these will surprise management and management must react positively. If the employees identify problems and want to fix them, let them and support their effort. Of course you will want to designate an individual or group of individuals to pass on all the ideas your employees come up with. You don't want all your employees going off and changing processes without some oversight. Remember that their way may not be your way; however, you should consider that if they do it their way they will be highly motivated to make it work—after all it was their idea. They surfaced the problem and came up with the fix.

- Examples of lower-level Mistake Proofing. Color coding, warning messages, alarms, work instructions, scales.

- Examples of higher-level Mistake Proofing. Bar-coding, comparative database, alphanumeric data checkers, photo eye, shape of a three-pronged plug. It is important that there be an understanding of the difference between a Lower-Level and an Upper-Level Mistake-Proofing solution because the work is never finished until an economical Upper-Level solution is found.

When trying to come up with a Mistake-Proofing solution, the participants should consider the following:

- Define the problem.

- Measure the effects of the problem including the cost.

- Identify the root cause of the problem.

- Find the best Mistake-Proofing method.

82

- Implement the method.

- Measure the results and establish a method to monitor the results.

- Present your Mistake-Proofing opportunity and solution.

Request that the participants breakout into small groups and work on Mistake Proofing the process problems they previously identified as possible in their area of work. The next day, have them return to the class with flipcharts detailing three things—the item they selected to Mistake Proof, how it will be Mistake Proofed and what the annual savings will be. After presenting, each presenter should commit to a date by which the project will be completed. If a project cannot be completed in less than two months, it is not right for this venue and should be tackled with a Self-Directed Team approach—see the next chapter. Most Mistake-Proofing projects will be completed in one to two weeks, many in less than a few days. Initially the solutions will be more Lower-Level than Higher-Level in nature. Over time, as the Teams' skills improve, the solutions will become increasingly Higher-Level.

Talk Up the Program: Posters, Newsletters, Etc.

Giving the Mistake-Proofing program some initial publicity and conveying ongoing results to the entire organization will further the cause. Use these tools to talk up the training so that by the time the trainees enter the classroom they will be eagerly anticipating the fun. Yes, the fun. They will enjoy the change of pace that will give them a measure of control over solving their everyday work problems, some for the first time. Your employees will feel more valuable and valued while you will give them the most empowering gift of all, knowledge!

Reward Good Work, Give Recognition and Celebrate Success

A rewards plan will be immensely helpful in gaining support for the program. It should be made clear at the outset that the rewards are not an attempt to compensate folks for their ideas and hard work. They are merely an expression of gratitude and recognition. The reward can be a small gift certificate, dinner for two, or a nice cash award, depending on the level of contribution. One company I consulted for with several locations did something different in each location. One location gave a $50 gift certificate for each idea implemented. Another gave employees a day off if their idea was used. Yet another gave a cash award that varied depending on the value of the contribution.

Recognition is a very important part of the reward system and for many it is more important than any monetary gift. It costs the company virtually nothing to recognize employee contributions, yet so many companies fail in this area. The program newsletter or area posters can be used to recognize contributors. Also, celebrations like pizza parties, company luncheons and picnics serve as good recognition occasions. All employee meetings and company-wide e-mails can serve to get the word out.

Don't forget to celebrate the program kickoff and major successes along the way. It can be as simple as cake and coffee or as elaborate as a formal party. Use your imagination or, better yet, let your Self-Directed Team use their imaginations, if you choose this form of program management.

Tracking Performance

All successes should be quantified and reported into a central point. The results should be published for all to see. Again, the Self-Directed Team can use this information as the basis for making awards and giving recognition. The savings can be impressive and the quality improvements can be great.

84

Collect the data and share the good news (See examples of tracking tools below).

PROJECT NUMBER	MISTAKE PROOFING PROJECTS IDENTIFIED	ASSIGNED PROJECT DATE	COMPLETION DATE

PROJECT NUMBER	LEAN MISTAKE PROOFING DASHBOARD PROJECT DESCRIPTION	TEAM NUMBER	MEASURE	OVERALL SAVINGS	ADDITIONAL EXPENSE	NET SAVINGS	COMPLETION DATE	PROJECT UPDATE

Chapter 5

Chapter 5

Self-Directed Cross-Functional Teams

For those initiatives that are too big in scope or would take too long to be accomplished using the Mistake-Proofing methods above, you should use the Cross-Functional Self-Directed Team. Use the talent you already have in place to meet your big challenges by setting stretch goals and by making the teams "Cross-Functional" to draw on the various talents across the organization.

Having a Team that crosses functional lines is expedient in that it will make available the diversity of talent that is usually required to address the initiatives that touch more than one area of the business. Another benefit derived from forming a Cross-Functional Team is its ability to eliminate resistance and to break down barriers at the grassroots level. By including as Team members individuals who are respected by their peers, the Team's ideas will be more readily accepted—the Team sells their ideas to their fellow employees that they interface with routinely. It may even be a good idea to include an individual on the Team who is believed to be resistant to this type of change. Eliminating resistance through Team membership is an excellent way to create a convert and converts will become the project zealots. Another good reason for forming a Cross-Functional Team is that it makes it easy to draw on the resources from an area of the business when one of the Team members is working in that area. Information Technology assistance is easier to secure if the person asking for the assistance is an employee from the Information Technology end of the business.

In addition to being "Cross-Functional," the Team is "Self-Directed." Self-directed means just that: self-directed. Most of us cannot rely on ourselves alone to accomplish major initiatives. It is usually necessary to draw on the talents of the people who surround us. The Team concept is far more effective without a dominating personality being present. Optimum Team performance is fostered when all Team members participate equally in the Team process. When all Team members feel that their opinions are important, they will give them freely. The senior member of management who forms the Team should pick the Team Leader and Team Facilitator, and then together with these individuals pick a few candidates for Team membership. At the first Team meeting after the Team has been formed, the senior manager forming the Team will address the group to deliver the challenge. After the Team challenge has been delivered, this individual leaves the Team meeting, not to return unless invited by the Team. Great care must be exercised by management not to interfere with the self-directed Team's work. This may even mean biting one's tongue and accepting what one believes to be a mistake in the interest of noninterference. Once an outsider with the power to interfere and to usurp the Team's authority does so, you no longer have a self-directed Team. If things are so bad that interference is absolutely necessary, request an invitation to address the Team and lay out your concerns. Make the Team understand that they are the decision-makers. Your guest appearance is just to make suggestions that the Team may elect to ignore. If your guest appearance fails to gain the desired results and greater interference is warranted, disband the Team and start over. At this point using your influence will neuter the Team anyway, so just start over with a fresh Team. Remember, responsibility, accountability and authority go together; you can't have one without the other two. A policy of

90

noninterference will make your self-directed Teams a powerful force in your business.

One of my actual experiences with a Cross-Functional Self-Directed Team that didn't take my advice involved my allowing the Team to spend a few thousand dollars more than they had to. Okay, I'll say it—allowing them to waste a few thousand dollars. The Team, when in the process of setting up a new data collection system, insisted on installing too many bar-code readers and printers. The Team wanted to place a reader and printer at the birthing station. This is the station that adds the initial bar-code to an item, giving it identity, and starts the clock ticking for the cycle time measurements. The Team also wanted readers at five other stations in the process. I requested and was granted an audience with the Team. I expressed my concern, telling the Team that when this area was converted, there would be no need for so many readers because the product would not be in the area long enough. The Team was playing the game under the current rules, by which the product remained in the area for weeks, not days or hours. I was drawing on my previous experiences, which told me that soon the crippling shortage situation would be cured and products would no longer take weeks to move through this area; it would take less than two days from the birthing station to the end of the line. I was eventually proven correct, but not before the Team purchased and installed every reader and printer they originally wanted. Obviously the Team was unmoved by my argument that the product would be moving so quickly through the area that the extra equipment would not be needed. They had lived for so many years with the shortage problems that they could not comprehend what life would be like without the shortages— their past experience dictated their actions.

I believe two things were going on in the above situation. First, the Team did believe that the equipment was needed. Second, the Team was testing whether management really meant what it said about the Teams being self-directed. Four different Cross-Functional Self-Directed Teams had been

91

simultaneously kicked off and this was the first test. If, at this early stage of Team empowerment, I had overruled the Team on its decision to purchase the equipment, the success of all the Teams would have been jeopardized. It was far better to spend a few extra dollars making an investment in the Team process than to undermine the Team's authority. Management gave the Teams the responsibility; management intended to hold the Teams accountable. It was necessary for management to reaffirm the Team's authority. All four Teams went on to be very successful, saving this company millions of dollars. The extra equipment was a good investment.

Influencing the Team

There are several ways for the Team's creator to influence the Team's performance. The first is through the Team Leader and the Team Facilitator, both of whom the Team's creator appointed when the Team was formed. The Team will generate minutes of each meeting. The minutes will be distributed not only to the Team members, but also to the Team's creator. In this way the Team's creator will know what direction the Team is taking. It is acceptable for the Team creator to attempt to influence both the Team Leader and the Team Facilitator, but not the Team members. The Facilitator should be skilled in dealing with conflict and should have the ability to deal with any conflicts that may arise in a professional manner. The Team creator, knowing that conflicts may arise between what the Team perceives is in the best interest of the organization and what management perceives is in the best interest of the organization, should pick the Facilitator carefully.

Another way for management to influence the Team is to set a date and call for a Team presentation. A very important element contributing to the success of the Cross-Functional Self-Directed Team concept is the Team presentation. The Team should be required to give periodic presentations to a member of the senior management Team on a regular basis. The stated purpose of the presentation will

92

be to update management on the Team's progress. The unstated purpose is to keep pressure on the Team to continue to make progress toward meeting the Team challenge. No one wants to get up in front of his or her management during the presentation and confess that the Team has not made any progress. There is a great deal of pressure from the Teammates themselves to "get stuff done" before the presentation date so that the Team can look good to management.

If the previous influencing methods are unsuccessful at moving the Team in the desired direction, the Team creator can request an invitation to attend a regular Team meeting or even call a special Team meeting. These should be very rare occasions. Too many of these requested audiences and you no longer have a Self-Directed Team. Present your best case to the Team, making them understand that you are not dictating to them, but also make it clear that you are trying to influence their decision, and then leave the meeting while the Team considers your suggestions.

In addition to the above you can always count on human nature. There is usually an inclination for the Team to want to please the Team's creator. So make your positions known. Keep the lines of communication between senior management and the Team open, upfront and honest. The Team will appreciate management giving them free rein in meeting the challenge. They will be inclined to please. And, of course, all Teams must operate within the existing company policies in force at the time.

Team Training

Soon after forming each new Team, provide the entire Team with formal Team training. Many human give leaders have had experience with Team training. If you have no one who can provide Team training inside your organization, this type of training is readily available through various human resource organizations.

93

The training should cover the various stages of Team development that most Teams go through from the kickoff stage through the productive stage. This will help the members understand what to expect in their interactions with their fellow Teammates. Other topics should include:

- Why governance is important.

- An understanding of what is expected of the Team Leader, the Team Facilitators and the Team members.

- An explanation of how the Team Leader's role changes as the Team matures. (The Team Leader assumes more of a Team member's role as the Team matures and leadership is no longer as necessary as it was when the Team was first formed.)

No role is more important here than the Team Facilitator's role. Unless the Team Facilitator already has experience and training in this role, it would be wise to provide facilitator training to the individuals serving in this role. Although a full member of the Team, the Facilitator has a unique role, in that his or her first responsibility is to the Team process itself. I usually try to get the Team Facilitators from the Human Resources group. These folks make good facilitators because they are far enough removed from routine day-to-day activities. A good Team Facilitator recognizes that his or her first responsibility is to monitor the Team process. The closer an individual is to the problem at hand, the more difficult it becomes to monitor the Team process. A trained Facilitator should be able to promote and encourage participation by all Team members, run interference with upper management, maintain fairness, help create a sense of harmony, keep the Team spirit alive, help settle internal disputes, recommend new Team members, and encourage the celebration of successes.

94

The Team Challenge

The Team challenge should be easy to understand, measurable, have a time limit and be relevant to the business's success. It should be a stretch to achieve, yet achievable. Some actual examples of Team challenges follow:

• Reduce the cost of mistakes by $800,000 over the next twelve months through the use of Mistake-Proofing methods.

• Train every employee on all levels in Mistake-Proofing methodology over the next ninety days.

• Reduce inventory by $10,000,000 by May 1.

• Implement a bar-coding system that tracks all orders from order to receipt by June 1.

Team Governance and Characteristics

I have listed below, with some elaboration, a few rules of governance and conduct that I have found successful in managing Cross-Functional Self-Directed Teams over the years.

• Team size should be more than five and less than twelve.

With fewer than five people you sacrifice the benefits of having a Cross-Functional or Self-Directed Team. Remember that one of the most powerful reasons for having such a Team is to gain acceptance in the affected areas; use too few people and you give up something here. More than twelve Team members and the Team is too unwieldy. There are too many group dynamics going on. It just gets too hard to keep everybody happy.

• Each Team is composed of a Team Leader—appointed; a Facilitator—appointed; a Secretary to keep minutes—elected; and the Team members—invited or drafted. This is pretty self-explanatory based on the discussions

95

above. If no one volunteers to take the minutes, the task can be rotated. The Team Leader and Facilitator should review the minutes before they are distributed.

•   The Team should meet at least once a week. Making this a ground rule forces the Team to meet and keep things moving. If the Team is meeting less than once a week, one has to question whether there is really a project going on or not. The first sign of trouble here will show up in the Team minutes or lack thereof.

•   When a Team accomplishes its goals and the challenge has been met, the Team will be disbanded. The on-going efforts can continue to be supported with the use of a steering committee, rather than a Cross-Functional Self-Directed Team. The Cross-Functional Self-Directed Teams should be used to define and execute major projects using the unique talents of the Team members. The work is usually over and above the Team members' everyday assignments; however, the challenge should be connected to the everyday work each Team member is normally assigned to do. In fact, it is best if the Team member will be a beneficiary of the successful Team outcome.

•   The Team must create an infrastructure that will survive the Team effort so that the accomplishments of the Team will continue to bear fruit long after the Team has been disbanded. In fact, the remaining infrastructure should outperform the Team that created it.

•   The Team sets goals and assigns tasks to meet the challenge. The Team creator establishes and delivers the challenge at the first Team meeting. However, the Team sets the goals that will have to be met to satisfy the challenge. In the case of a Self-Directed Team it would be counterproductive and presumptuous for the creator to set the Team's goals. The nature of the ongoing dynamics involved in the Teamwork will dictate changing goals as the Team progresses in its work. It would not be practical to have a Self-

Directed Team and have the Team creator set the goals. This would negate the self-direction aspect of the Team.

• The Team is empowered to draw on the talents and expertise available elsewhere in the company. This includes the entire organization. The talent would most likely be required on a part-time basis. For example, if help is required from the Sourcing group to get vendor quotes for posters and promotional materials, a buyer will be assigned to the Team until the quoting is complete. In this case it would make no sense for the Buyer to become a full Team member for the duration of the Team's existence, so a temporary assignment will serve the Team well. One note here: when the time comes to hand out the rewards for the Team's successes, don't forget to include the part-timers proportionally for their efforts.

• Team meeting attendance and showing up on time are both important and mandatory in order to maintain Team membership. The Team must establish these ground rules early on, in the first or second meeting. It is a must that all Team members understand the rules. The entire Team must agree to the boundaries. Consequences for noncompliance must be established and adhered to. So many Teams fail to address these difficult issues at the outset, and then when a member starts missing meetings or letting the Team down in some way, the Team has no recourse. The Team creator should place a strong emphasis on the ground rule-setting needs at the kickoff meeting when the challenge is delivered. The Facilitator, especially if he or she is a human resource professional, can help with this process.

One Team's actual experience involving a Team member who continually let the Team down drove the Team to fire the individual from the Team. This individual served on two Teams and eventually the process was repeated with the other Team as well. Not long after being dismissed from the second Team, the individual left the company. These Teams both went on to become very successful despite this episode. The separation from the Team was handled professionally, partly because the mechanism was in place, having been dealt with at the Team's inception. The Team's ability to terminate a Team member from the Team can be a powerful motivator. Most people would prefer to be fired by their company than to be fired by their peers.

• Teams are expected to give progress reports in the form of a presentation to a senior member of management, the more senior the better. The presentation helps to keep the project on track. It is the ultimate in Team pressure. The peer pressure to be prepared to deliver a good presentation is awesome. Nobody wants to go before top management unprepared or with little to show for the Team's effort.

• This is the Team's opportunity to show off their abilities. They have a captive audience, a chance to get top management to listen. I have seen wondrous things happen during Team presentations. There is some real give and take that goes on in these meetings. A Team in need of additional resources may ask for management's commitment after trying to convince management that the Team is worthy of further investment. It is impressive to see the effort that most Teams put into their presentations. They usually surprise on the upside with their command of the issues surrounding their project. Some of the presentations are on the lighter side, and as such create an atmosphere of excitement and fun. Remember, every Team member should participate to some degree.

• Other governance ground rules should be established at the outset, at the first or second meeting, by the Team. We have already talked quite a bit about the importance of this action. Issues to be addressed include missing meetings without an excuse, being regularly late for meetings, consequences, majority rule, open vote versus closed vote, level of expected effort, procedure for adding or removing members, frequency of meetings and any other issues the Team deems it necessary to cover. The Team creator should reinforce the importance of establishing these ground rules

98

early. He should explain that although it is hoped that the mutual respect the Team members have for each other will be enough to resolve any issues that come up, it is good business practice to formalize the ground rules governing Team activities and behavior, if only to avoid any misunderstanding.

Team Celebrations and Awards

Celebrations are a great way to say thanks and to encourage more of the same results that will bring more celebrations. Celebrate even the small successes. They can be as simple as a cake and coffee break or a pizza party. The acknowledgement of a job well done is the important thing. Just say thanks. Companies with more resources can do more—cash awards, gift certificates, etc.

In addition to the minor celebrations along the Team's path to meeting the challenge, one of my companies gave each Team member a $1,000 cash award and the Team Leader received $1,500 for his or her efforts. Yet another company I was involved with gave each employee a check for $250 each time the Team gave a presentation to top management. This in no way was meant as compensation for the work they had done. In most cases it would not have amounted to fifty cents an hour in compensation for all the extra hours the Team members put in on the projects. The awards were a way to say thanks for their efforts. It was as much a bonus for their spouses, who sacrificed while their husbands or wives worked extra time. On one occasion, several members from a Team in Connecticut were asked to spend Valentine's Day in Milwaukee, Wisconsin. The Team Leader had roses sent to the Team members' spouses back in Connecticut. What a hit that was; they talked about that gesture for months. Another Team had the company cafeteria prepare dinners to be taken home for the spouses of the Team members who had to work late on a project. This only cost the company a few dollars per person and demonstrated to the Team members' families that the company recognized

99

and was appreciative of the sacrifice the whole family was making in order to help create a stronger, more secure employment situation for all involved. It made the employees look like heroes in their families' eyes.

Some Teams would give away leather binders with the Team's name on the cover. Others would have ball caps or jackets. This was a way for the Team members to build Team spirit, and to identify and be identified with their Team. Evening mystery cruises, dinner theatre tickets, baseball tickets, you name it and these Teams did it. They worked hard and had fun doing it.

Benefits of Cross-Functional Self-Directed Teams

One of the nicest benefits of forming Cross-Functional Self-Directed Teams is their ability to break down traditional barriers between departments. Team members are placed in situations where they have to rely and depend on each other's talents and skills to succeed as a Team. There is nothing like these types of situations to generate respect for fellow employees. Just becoming familiar with a co-worker's responsibilities and daily challenges brings an understanding between individuals and groups. Development of mutual respect is a natural byproduct of an entire Team drawn from different areas of the business, pulling in the same direction to achieve a common goal.

Improved communications is another Team benefit. Communications between individuals and organizations can't help but improve when fellow employees sit next to each other working on a common goal. Remember the Team must meet at least once a week.

The Cross-Functional Self-Directed Teams will foster camaraderie and the goodwill created will far outlast the Teams or their efforts. After all, many have learned a new common lingo through their Teamwork. The friendships and relationships developed through the Teamwork will spill over into the other day-to-day activities in the rest of the business. Some of the relationships between employees even spill over into their personal lives. In some of my companies there were very strong personal relationships that continued for years after the Team effort was over. They joined professional organizations together and some went to school together at night.

Employees develop a sense of ownership when asked to resolve a major issue that deeply affects the company's success. The project becomes their baby. They want to see that nothing adverse happens to negatively affect their baby. And, of course, when a Team member gets close to a project, they are getting closer to the entire company. The more they have invested in a company, the keener they are about the health of that company.

We end up with better, longer-lasting improvements that are implemented much more quickly. With limited resources, where does a company get the talent they need to run the day-to-day business while at the same time making great improvements on a grand scale? The answer is the Cross-Functional Self-Directed Team.

The MAGIC

There is magic in a Self-Directed Team. As a matter of fact, there are three forms of magic. First, the Team has the power to fire Team members. That puts great pressure on the Team members to perform. We all have been on Teams where among eight members, three do all the work. That can't happen on a Self-Directed Team. The risk of being fired by your peers is too great. The second form of magic is the requirement to do a presentation for top management. Who wants to tell their top management that they have been working on a problem for months and haven't accomplished anything? The third form is the magic of a quantified objective.

No Work Happens Until the Tool Hits the Material

Use these Teams to get the work done. One thing I remember from my college physics classes—no work happens until the tool hits the material. You get up in the morning, shower, dress, eat breakfast and drive to your place of work. You may get a cup of coffee. Collect your tools or lay out the work you need to do in front of you. Up to this point, NO WORK HAS HAPPENED. Not until you pick up the tool—be it pencil, pen, or screwdriver—and touch it to the material, has any work happened. Once the tool has touched the material, then you can claim that work has happened. Your Cross-Functional Self-Directed Teams are your tools. Your challenges are their work. Your job as creator is to bring them together.

Examples of Self-Directed Teams

Reduce inventory by $10,000,000 by the end of the year. This was the challenge of an Inventory Reduction Team. The Team was very successful. They started with $24,000,000 in inventory and successfully reduced that inventory to $14,000,000. In actuality there were three distinct Teams in this same company, which served in succession. The three Teams eventually drove inventory down to $7,000,000, while at the same time top line revenue doubled, making the inventory investment work more than six times harder than it had prior to the Teams' work.

The second Inventory Reduction Team was formed after the first Team was disbanded, and the third Team was formed after the second Team was disbanded. A Cross-Functional Self-Directed Team should be disbanded with celebration when it has met its challenge. If this were not the case, the Teams would go on forever, tying up valuable resources that should be focused elsewhere. Three different

102

Teams were required because, although the goal of reducing inventory was common to all three Teams, the methods they had to use to achieve their goals were quite different. Hence, three different Teams were composed of people with different talents, who were able to deal with the different issues facing each of the three Teams. For instance, the first Team focused on issues like selling used inventory equipment, reworking unusable inventory into usable inventory and then selling it, and returning unneeded material to the vendors who supplied it or pushing off material deliveries by rescheduling purchase orders. There were Team members from Sales and Marketing to help move the inventory, as well as members from areas of the business to help figure out how to repair and rework unusable inventory into usable inventory. By the time the last of the three Inventory Reduction Teams started their work, they were focusing on things like reducing the size of the material Kanbans and integrating assemblies. The makeup of the final Team didn't include any members from Sales or Marketing; its membership centered on the supply chain.

Improve on-time delivery hit rate to the 99 percent+ level over the next year. This Team was coming from so far behind that it actually took almost a year and a half to satisfy the challenge. On-time delivery was at 53 percent when the Team challenge was delivered. Also, some of the late orders were weeks late, not just a few days. The company was shipping more than 10,000 line items a month to virtually every hospital in the United States and many outside the USA. An order was considered on time if it was shipped prior to the promised ship date. No tolerance window was allowed. If the order was one minute late, it was counted as late. Prior to the Team's measurement of on-time delivery for the first time, this company didn't even know how bad its delivery rate was.

The Team's members came from the various areas of the Company that had the most influence over on-time delivery, including: Order Entry, Customer Service, Sales, Shipping/Logistics, Sourcing and Manufacturing, while the

Facilitator was the Human Resources Manager. These Team members addressed and improved a variety of issues that were causing late deliveries, such as: unrealistic promises to customers, late vendor deliveries causing late builds, priority setting, freight carrier selection, short shipments, order entry errors and customer ordering errors.

When the Team was disbanded, they left behind a strong infrastructure that would build on their successes for years to come. Eventually, on-time delivery was defined as the date the customer requested the delivery at the customer's site. This is a much tougher method of measuring on-time delivery, basing performance on the date the customer wants the delivery, rather than on the date you promised the delivery. When you know you are being measured, you tend to pad the delivery promise. With the new tougher measure the customer can be unreasonable and the measurement stands—meet the request and you are on time, miss the request and you are late. Also, early shipments were not allowed and partial shipments were not allowed.

Improve on-time delivery from 75 percent to 99 percent over the next five months. This consumer products company was about to lose its biggest customer for one of its key product lines. The customer, the largest retailer in the USA, insists that their suppliers maintain a high degree of on-time delivery. If the shelf space reserved for the product is empty, it could be filled with a competitor's product. The Team put Kanban techniques in place both internally and externally to resolve many of the issues causing the poor performance. Meeting the challenge restored on-time delivery to the 99 percent+ level and saved the customer relationship.

Reduce purchase costs for services and materials by $3,000,000 annualized, over the next ten months. When my partner and I first visited this client to interview the key employees, we were told that the purchase cost savings goal for the next year was $75,000. The annual spend for services and material was $40,000,000—not a very aggressive goal. A few weeks later we started a Self-Directed Team and gave them a challenge of saving $3,000,000 over the next ten months. At first they looked at each of us like we had two heads, but they soon accepted the challenge after being assured that the task was very doable. Their previous goal of $75,000 did not require much imagination—just some negotiation with their suppliers. The new stretch challenge of $3,000,000 required that they change their approach rather than just negotiate with suppliers; they had to think about what they made in-house and what they purchased outside and rationalize each decision. In addition, they looked at reducing warehouse space, reducing insurance and transportation, as well as other costs. The results were amazing. The $3,000,000 challenge was met in six months not ten. In ten months they had saved $4,000,000 and in a year and a half they had saved a total of $8,000,000.

Reduce floor space requirements by 50 percent within the next year. This Team actually reduced floor space by more than 50 percent within the year. They converted the facility to a pull Kanban system with point-of-use delivery and required some partnering suppliers to deliver directly to customers. These efforts eliminated virtually all warehousing and storage requirements.

Streamline new product introduction process so that 100 percent of new products are introduced on time and within budget in the next eight months. Product introduction was always a challenge for this business as they suffered from short product life cycles. New products made up much of this business's annual revenue. They seldom introduced products on time and almost never within budget. This Team was so successful that the company introduced 105 new products on time and within budget the following year.

Relocate the business from Burlington, Massachusetts to Connecticut in the next sixty days. This Team used the pitcher-catcher approach. The catcher was the group receiving the business in Connecticut and the pitcher was the group moving the business from Massachusetts. A Self-

105

Directed Team proved to be an excellent method of managing this move. Not a single customer commitment was missed.

Automate the data collection system and have the new system up and running by January 1. This Team suffered through three different Leaders. The first died, the second quit and the third remained until the Team was disbanded. This Team effort not only suffered through three different Team Leaders, it was a victim of project creep. As the Team was about to wrap up the original project and declare the challenge met, the parent company decided to implement a new global ERP system. Of course, this meant that much of the original interface work with the current system had to be done over. It was felt that the Team in place was the closest to the issues and would have the best chance at succeeding with the interface to the new ERP system. Many new requirements were added to the specification to take advantage of the new system's capabilities. The software that the Team had originally selected did not play well with the new system, leading to several ugly workaround solutions. None of these difficulties were the fault of the Team; however, their spirits were dampened and the work dragged on with little to celebrate. Eventually the Team delivered on most of the requirements, but it took years—far too long for a Self-Directed Team. In retrospect, it would have been far better to sacrifice any benefit derived from the Team's experience with the first iteration of the automated data collection system and start a new Team with the introduction of the global ERP system. A valuable lesson for all involved to remember.

This Team had a very large membership: a dozen members. The specialized knowledge each Team member had in his or her respective areas dictated the need for a large Team. Also, as this system's effect was far-reaching in the organization, the Team's membership was drawn from those many areas most affected in an effort to ensure buy-in.

One more thought on this Team: the presentations the Team delivered to top management were superb. Initially the Team had an unbelievable amount of spirit. During one of the

106

presentations delivered to the President of the company and members of his staff, the Team did a skit involving every member of the Team. The theme centered on the tons of paper that the Team would be eliminating from the business. They collected one month's worth of paper and filled several carts. Wheeling the carts into the conference room drove home the importance of the Team's work. It was a very effective presentation.

Eliminate all obsolete part numbers in the system within the next six months. This was the challenge of the "Part Number Elimination Team." This Team's job was to clean up the part number system that had been in effect for several decades and transferred from one business system to another. The Team eliminated part numbers that were no longer needed because they were obsolete or in some cases duplicates. One characteristic that stood out with this Team was its ZEAL. The Team would routinely work through lunch performing the tedious tasks of investigating each part number that was a candidate for elimination. They would order pizzas and eat while they worked on their own time.

Chapter 6

Chapter 6

The Workout Process

The Workout Process combines the change acceleration process and gap analysis to arrive at a go-forward consensus plan that can be quickly put in motion to achieve a desired result. We have used this approach to: put in place a plan to implement a division-wide "enterprise resource planning" business system; resolve conflicts between senior managers; develop strategic business plans to rescue failing businesses; dramatically remove costs from individual areas of businesses; restructure and reform trouble-causing business functions within organizations; reduce millions of dollars in the costs of goods and services; and, after Hurricane Katrina, we used this technique to develop a plan quickly to ramp up production of hydrogen in the Northeast since much of the nation's hydrogen production facilities were under water. Hydrogen is necessary for manufacturing metals, cooling gas turbines in power plants and powering fuel cells, as well as for many other applications. Hydrogen is a necessity without practical substitutes.

The objective of the Workout process is to come up with a _consensus plan,_ which contains action steps, an action owner assigned to each action step and a timeline commitment that when executed well will lead to a successful

111

outcome. It is necessary first to define the *current state*—the actual conditions right now, today, so that everyone involved in the Workout has the same understanding of where you are starting from. The next step is to define the *desired state*, or future state: where do you want to end up after the consensus plan is executed?

Select the Facilitator carefully. He or she should be someone who is a well-respected person in the organization or someone from outside the business who has experience facilitating this type of process. Holding the session off-site is preferable in order to limit the possibility of interruptions and to keep the group focused. It is recommended that flipcharts be used to record the current state. Hang the flipcharts on the wall for reference. When moving from the current state to defining the desired state, do the same thing—use flipcharts to record the items and hang them on an opposing wall. To build a consensus plan, consider the actions necessary to move from the current state to the desired state. Brainstorming is a particularly helpful process for coming up with actions required to achieve the desired state. Record the action steps necessary to achieve the desired state, and assign responsibility and commitment dates to each of the action items. Only high-level action steps are necessary during the actual Workout. After the Workout session, the action steps can be expanded to come up with a detailed action plan for each element of the consensus plan. A "risk analysis" should be done to identify potential risks with your plans. Steps to mitigate each serious risk identified should be taken.

The techniques for running a Workout are simple, easy to understand, and can be mastered relatively quickly. This makes this tool ideal for any-sized business or any-sized business problem that fits the circumstances best served by this process.

The first step in the process is to define the "current state." That is the way things really are right now. If your goal

112

is to develop a strategic business plan, you must first define the current state of the business. In fact, let us use the development of a strategic business plan as an example to describe the Workout process here. All involved in the Workout should agree as to what the current state of the business actually is. The current state can be defined in terms of numbers, organization charts, process maps, or any other device that conveys the current state of the business. Revenue, net profit, margin, bank line performance, growth rates, budget performance and other financial data will be helpful. Other can include compensation plan, inventory analysis, ranking talent levels, customer service level, current markets served, quality of product/service, competition, product life cycles, existing cost savings programs, an analysis of the technology (including use of the Internet) and systems used in the business, process issues, sales promotions and advertising, prevailing morale, and current vision statement. Add to the foregoing anything that helps define the current condition of the business.

It is not absolutely necessary to have each item defined to the last penny or last letter; however, it is important that the information be at least directionally correct. Information can be further corroborated after the initial Workout to work out each detail. Remember, we are trying to put together an action plan that everyone involved agrees to, so that we can move forward. Part of that consensus plan can be further defining some of the assumptions used to develop the plan. If you wait until you collect every last bit of data, you may end up doing nothing.

Once you have defined the current state of the business and it is the general consensus of the group, you can move on to define the "desired state." What do you want the business to look like in the future? To do this you can refer to the way you defined the current state for hints at areas that need or could use improvement. Add to this any other changes that would be an improvement in the business. You

113

might, for example, want to increase the top and bottom line performance and/or the level of management talent. Make these things part of your desired state definition. When all agree on the desired state definition, you can move on to building your consensus action plan with action owners and timeline commitments.

I suggest that you use some type of software that will make it easy to keep track of the progress you are making toward meeting your goal. I personally like Microsoft Project. Project lets you link dependent tasks, allowing you to see readily the effects of falling behind on a related task. You can also keep track of required resources. The software is pretty user-friendly and easily mastered.

In the above example of constructing a business plan, the company was able to put together a plan that led to new, realistic, achievable financial goals; store closings in unprofitable locations; new store openings in profitable locations; and a plan to upgrade employee talent, just to name a few of the actions that came out of this effort that took only a few days.

Other Examples of Successful Workouts

Implement a Division-Wide Enterprise Resource Planning System

This was a division of a major corporation that had dozens of different business systems. The business systems were inherited when companies were acquired and merged into the division. This made intercompany transactions difficult. You can imagine what rolling up the financials from dozens of different business systems at the end of month looked like. The Workout involved seven people, who came up with a high-level consensus plan to move this business to one business system that works very efficiently to this day. This plan was developed in less than one day. Of course, the Workout process was second nature to the management in this business—it was used regularly to develop actionable plans.

Resolve Conflicts Between Senior Managers

This process can be used to resolve conflicts between members of management. By its nature, the process of putting together a consensus plan drives the players to work together to reach a common goal. Together they define the current state, come up with the desired state and then create a consensus plan to arrive at the desired state. This is a great way to get your people to work together.

Reduce the Cost of Goods and Services by $5 Million

This Workout took place in Washington State. When we arrived, the goal for cost savings was $500,000 over the next year. When asked how the savings were to be achieved, no one had any answers. A formal plan was a foreign concept to this group. Three days later, after a Workout involving a cross-functional group of employees, they had a consensus plan to save millions of dollars. The plan identified just how the savings were to be achieved with individuals signed up for each task, which was committed to a timeline. They raised their hands and made commitments to each other. Vendors were identified, redesigns were committed to, plans were made to bring some items in-house as well as to subcontract other items that were done in-house and material substitutions were suggested for review. Actual savings over the next year amounted to over $5,000,000.

115

Packaging Issues Resolved

This company in New Jersey had many serious packaging issues that went unresolved. Finger-pointing was the order of the day in this organization. The solution was to get everyone involved in a Workout. This Workout included over twenty people—a larger group than normal. At the start of the session everyone was pointing at each other; everything that was wrong with packaging in this company was someone else's fault. After the first few hours, everyone realized that there was not an innocent player in the room. All had contributed to the problem in some way. The session was cathartic. Only after everyone had a clear understanding of the current state could they move on and solve the packaging problems—which they were then able to do.

Chapter 7

Chapter 7

Flexibility

Material Flexibility and Inventory Productivity

One of the most important business goals is to create as much flexibility as possible with material, labor and equipment. Flexibility allows us to make quick adjustments to business conditions, such as schedules and material requirements, which gives us the ability to react to sudden changes in plans—increases or decreases—without the need to keep large stores of inventory on hand. This ability, coupled with high product throughput velocity—moving work-in-process and finished goods quickly to our customers—will keep overall inventory at a minimum. More inventory is _not_ the way to create flexibility. On the contrary, establishing vendor relationships that require you to keep less inventory is the answer—you don't want more inventory, you want the right inventory delivered to you when you need it. Productivity is measured by how efficiently we use our labor, equipment and material. If we could cut all the material employed in business in the USA in half, then we would be able to double the productivity of that material investment. This is a goal I hope that you will come to believe is very modest after you finish reading this book. To use an economics cliché, improving productivity raises all the boats. The added wealth generated by doubling the productivity of inventories in the entire USA would surely lead to a very dramatic improvement in the nation's economic health.

In this section we will deal with material flexibility. In short, always have what you need when you need it and not before. On your end, you don't care when your vendor makes it. All you care about is that he or she has what you need and can get it to you when you need it.

Try to share as many of your inventory problems with your vendors as you possibly can by not taking ownership of the inventory until just before you are about to use it or ship it to your customer. This will encourage your suppliers to come up with new solutions and methods to help you lower your inventory.

The in-house stores. In this scenario your vendor owns the inventory until you draw it out of the store. Even then, you may make a payment arrangement with your vendor to pay for the goods in sixty days or more. In one of my more recent companies, the product was built, shipped, and in some cases we had even collected payment for the goods from the customers before the vendor was paid. A good deal for our company; our vendors were helping to finance the operation. Similarly, consignment inventory acts in the same manner. This is your vendor's inventory, which is consigned to your care until you draw on it. When you use it, you notify your vendor; at that point you take ownership and the material moves into your inventory. The key difference between an in-house store and consignment inventory is that you are responsible for the care of the consignment inventory while it is in your facility. Any loss or damage is your responsibility. In an in-house store the vendor's own employees manage and keep track of their own inventory. Anything that happens to cause an inventory loss prior to your drawing the material from the in-house store is your vendor's problem, not yours.

Next is the "Bread Man routine." Here, too, you can get your vendor to help you by negotiating the right deal. In one of our German operations we had negotiated an arrangement with a key vendor to supply hardware, wire and small-machined parts. As the material was removed from the vendor's designated area by our employees, a part number was entered into a PC which was integrated with a counting scale. The parts were placed on the counting scale. Each single part's weight was known by the integrated weighing system. The quantity being removed from the vendor's stock was calculated and downloaded to the vendor's system and our system simultaneously. At the end of each month, our accounts payable folks would transfer payment on the negotiated date to satisfy the vendor's accounts receivable. It was the vendor's responsibility to keep the bins in our business that held their material full. Obviously a certain level of trust must exist between you and your vendor for this to work. This is just one variation of the "Bread Man routine." The possibilities are virtually endless and you are limited only by your imagination. Again, using these techniques, it is easy to see how you could collect payment for products you have shipped to your customer before you have to pay your vendor for the material used.

And lastly, we have the Kanbans or Wand-to-order method. Here you have very little material in your inventory, provided your vendors are delivering in small enough quantities. Hopefully, you have no more than a few days' supply of material, at least for those items supplied by your local vendors. Here, too, you can negotiate favorable payment terms with your vendors, and again it is possible to collect payment from your customers before you have to pay your vendors for the material you sold your customers.

Partnering With Your Vendors

Here is as good a place as any to talk about partnering with your vendors. It is pretty easy to take advantage of your vendor's desire to capture a nice piece of business from you, their customer. But the relationship won't last unless there is something in it for both you and your vendor. The only good deal is a deal where both parties win.

I realize that much of what has been said so far about the various methods of taking deliveries of inventory from your suppliers could sound like heavy-handedness. You must always be careful to guard against this kind of behavior in your organization. If at all possible, you want to avoid even the perception of heavy-handedness in dealing with your suppliers. If unfairness is allowed, you will have very short-term gains for a while, and then ultimately you will fail. No vendor will tolerate being taken advantage of for any longer than he or she has to. Eventually, your prices will go up or your vendor will start to miss deliveries in favor of devoting his or her resources to other, more profitable customers. Alternatively, the quality of the material will start to slip as your vendor cuts corners in an effort to recoup some of the lost profits. Somehow you will end up paying a heavy price for taking advantage of your relationship with your vendor. Teach your buyers and Sourcing Leaders to partner with your vendors. Insist on it! Accept nothing less than the highest ethical standards of behavior in your Sourcing group.

In one of my businesses, we were doing business with a local vendor who manufactured wooden cabinets that we sold as a third-party item with our equipment. The cabinets were offered more to please our customers' desire for one-stop shopping than to produce profits. They were being sold for close to cost, around $400. This local vendor refused to deliver on a demand-pull basis, claiming that he was a small operation and needed to deliver when the cabinets were finished, no matter what the requested delivery date was. After several attempts to work with this vendor failed, my Sourcing Manager started looking for another source of supply. The search, which was initiated in an attempt to find a vendor who would deliver on a demand-pull basis, also yielded a cost savings of around 30 percent, making this product now profitable. One problem was that the vendor was not local. He was located in the Midwest. My Sourcing Manager and my Logistics Manager worked out a great deal with this Midwest supplier whereby the supplier would drop ship directly to our customer upon receipt of a faxed copy of one of our customer's orders. After the supplier trained their employees to fill our customers' orders, this process worked well for years.

The local vendor we had been using was devastated. They had believed that our many protests at the way they did business were just so many attempts to squeeze them for price reductions and get them to hold our inventory. We brought them in and laid out the new deal we had with our new vendor in the Midwest. They admitted to us, and more importantly to themselves, that because of the way they currently ran their business, they could not have matched the deal even if they had taken us at our word that we would have to find another vendor to replace them. They had to change or go out of business. The story does not end here.

A few months later I happened to be in the Midwest and decided to call on this vendor to see how they were doing with our cabinets. We had given them a large blanket order for 1,200 cabinets. Our history showed that the sales for these cabinets were pretty linear. We averaged five a day; some days we may have shipped none, other days we could ship ten or even fifteen, but almost never would we ship more than fifteen. When we went for a tour of their shop, they were pleased to show us the four hundred cabinets they had nearing completion and further boasted about the material they had on hand for the next four hundred. I was stunned. In this setup, they could have built the cabinets very efficiently in lots of twenty-five. Then the owner of this privately owned company showed me his warehouse with well over a million dollars of material in stock, mostly readily available lumber. I

123

knew that to be able to maintain a successful and long-lasting relationship with this supplier, we had to help him understand more about material management.

I started by asking him if there were great quantity discounts for the lumber he bought. There were, but they were not significant enough to justify the carrying cost. I asked if he thought he could get his suppliers to accept large orders at the prices he was currently paying, but deliver and bill on short notice. He was sure he could arrange this; after all, the supplier was close by and delivered daily. Then I next asked him if he would like an extra million dollars in his bank account. The light came on. I assigned a Sourcing Manager to work with his company, educating them on Kanban pull techniques. This supplier went on to serve us well over the next several years, delivering cost reductions and performing further added-value services. This relationship made our company a lot of money on cabinet sales in the following years, an item we had carried and sold at close to breakeven just to satisfy the one-stop shopping demands of a few customers. Another win-win for all.

On occasion, for the good of all parties involved, you do need to be forceful in your relationship with your vendors. When necessary, this should be done with the purest of motives. You can hardly ever go too far wrong when you are being aggressive with your vendor for the right reasons. Eventually the vast majority of our vendors were convinced to deliver goods based on some form of a Kanban pull system. Although they were resistant at first, they came to realize (sometimes with a push) that they could use these techniques as a competitive advantage by offering the same services to other customers. Yes, at first our Sourcing Managers were forced to put it on the line—get on board or we will be forced to shop elsewhere. Once our vendors got on the bandwagon, it wasn't long before they were coming up with unique ways to deliver material, based on their own version of the Kanban pull system.

Velocity

Velocity, how long it takes to move product through your business, is every bit as important as the methods used to bring material into your business. If you have a month's supply of a particular product and it takes a month to get the product to your customers, then you are turning that inventory twelve times per year. You are getting twelve turns on those committed assets. One way to double your turns on these inventory assets is to cut your cycle time in half, or, to put it another way, increase your velocity to two weeks for this product and this will then give you twenty-six turns annually. Better yet, improve your processes so that the cycle time is reduced to one week and you will be at fifty-two turns per year. Nice improvement and your material assets for this product are now more than four times as productive as they were when you started with a turn of twelve. This is a very achievable and worthy goal.

Improvement in velocity starts when you start to measure it. Most companies don't even know what their throughput velocity is. The sensor-producing department in one of my factories was able to reduce inventory from $262,000 to less than $18,000 by converting their system from a work order push system to a Kanban pull system and changing some of their methods of making the product. In this instance the methods changes included: 1. Converting to UV-cured epoxies, eliminating the time and temperature curing wait time. 2. Bringing part of the process, which had previously been outsourced, in-house in order to eliminate the vendor's operation time, queue time and the travel time to and from the outside vendor. These actions resulted in a better than 93 percent reduction in inventory. Some of these sensors, prior to the changes, used to remain in process for as long as six weeks. After the changes to a Kanban pull system, all sensors were completed in no longer than eight hours.

Dealing With Low Cost Country (LCC) Suppliers

Another important consideration when dealing with very long supply chains such as Low Cost Country Suppliers in places such as China, India, and Eastern Europe, is the amount of safety stock you need to carry. The types of issues that must be taken into consideration are missed or cancelled flights, other shipping delays, customs clearance time, government agency inspections, holidays, etc. Every attempt should be made to move the responsibility for controlling these issues to your LCC suppliers. One answer is to have your LCC suppliers contract with a freight forwarder located near your operation to deal with importing, clearance and warehousing issues. Then the material can be pulled into your operation with a Kanban signal. Under these circumstances your LCC supplier takes the responsibility for carrying the necessary safety stock. In this way, the supplier will be highly motivated to execute well on his end to avoid problems on your end, making the safety stock requirement minimal. After all, your supplier has more control over the supply chain than you do, and it makes sense for the one with the most control to have the most responsibility in getting the goods to you when you need them.

Other Inventory Flexibility Considerations

There are many other inventory flexibility ideas that should at least be considered in any good inventory reduction program. A few of my favorites are covered below:

- Kanban size reduction. Kanbans should be constantly reviewed for ways to reduce Kanban size. There should be an annual reduction goal established that Operations and Sourcing Leaders commit to.

- Never accept early deliveries. It does not take long to train your vendors to refrain from unauthorized early delivery. Most business systems can identify and reject early shipments on receipt. You have two ways to deal effectively with this problem. The first is to refuse all early shipments. The second is to accept the early shipment and hold the payment while communicating with the vendor that his payment will be held because of his early delivery.

- Expedite returning material to your vendors (RTV material). Busy buyers tend to let these issues slide. This area always seems to be a problem. Evaluate your buyers on how quickly they deal with these issues. A very visible designated area labeled with the responsible buyer's name will also help manage this issue. Make sure each person involved in the process understands that this material is on your books.

- Coordinate new product introductions very carefully with the Marketing and Sales organizations. If your Sales organization starts to take orders for the new product before material unique to the old product is consumed, you will be stuck with obsolete goods. Also, Sales personnel must be careful about the timing of announcements for the release of a new product. If they announce too early, customers may wait to buy and you will be stuck with material for the old product. Again, education is the key here. Educate those involved with new product introductions, giving them a clear understanding of the impact on inventory, especially how this can affect future product costs, which will result in increasing their customers' prices and making your products less competitive.

Be very careful how you recognize the value of returned goods. Make sure you don't take them back into your inventory at a value greater than you can resell them for. If you are taking a worthless piece of equipment back in trade on a new sale, write it off on return. Better yet, identify and write it off as a discount on the sale—that is what it really is—and be sure to reduce the sales commission by the value of the worthless returned goods. Don't pay taxes on false earnings in one period only to have to write off the returned goods in another financial period; you will just be kidding yourself, and soon you won't be able to tell which segments of your business are profitable and which ones are not. You need to understand the effects of your inventory decisions on your operation's profitability. Another caution: don't pay sales commissions for goods that are returned when a customer decides not to keep the product. This will only encourage more borderline sales that don't stick.

- Control your demo inventory closely. Keep your demo inventory turning over. If at all possible, have your Sales people sell their demo equipment in the field, turning it over often. It is usually far better to sell your demo equipment at a deep discount than to write it off because it is too old to sell. Caution: be on the lookout for demo equipment that has turned into a gift. Analyze the age and whereabouts of your demo equipment to reveal product that is carried as demo, but really has been out on a long-term loan or even gifted—sanctioned or not. This equipment should be dealt with, either billed for or expensed.

- Fire sale obsolete product early or off-load it to a used equipment dealer. The earlier you deal with it, the bigger the return will be. Few products increase in value when they age unless they reach antique status. Unless you are in the antique business, make time to deal with these issues early. Write it off or gift it to schools and take the tax deduction to lower your taxes.

- Finally, any item that is not part of your core competency should be considered for outsourcing. Be careful here; do not outsource items that will increase your product cycle time.

Creating Equipment Flexibility Capacity

In most cases, overall equipment flexibility as it relates to capacity is a given. The majority of companies are working one eight-hour shift, five days a week, augmented by a small amount of overtime when necessary. This means that the equipment is sitting idle sixteen hours a day during the five-day work week and twenty-four hours a day on most weekends. There is a great deal of capacity and flexibility in that idle time.

The extra labor cost to take advantage of the additional capacity on an overtime basis is much less than you would think at first glance. If you are paying your employees time and a half after the first forty hours (or after eight hours in a day in some cases), this cost for overtime is almost a wash in most companies and can even be less costly in others. When you compare the cost of overtime to the cost of adding new people, overtime can look pretty inexpensive. First, you have benefits such as medical insurance, dental insurance, life insurance, 401K matches, pension expense, etc. In many companies these add up to 40 percent or more of the base pay. Second, often you do not pay for break time when employees work overtime. If employees work one or two hours overtime, they usually don't take any additional breaks. Third, there are no additional training costs associated with the folks who work overtime. Your overtime workers already know how to do their jobs. They are the same reliable workers who are already working for you during the regular work day. When you consider all the required training—not only the training associated with building and delivering your product or service, but also other required training such as environmental health and safety training — the training bill can be huge. Fourth, you save on backroom expenses such as payroll,

129

accounting, human resource record maintenance, employment taxes, etc. Last but not least, you usually pick the most reliable and productive workers to work overtime, so you should get the best on an overtime basis. Even if you have a Union Shop and are required to rotate overtime, the best workers are usually the ones who want the extra work, while the ones with less energy usually turn down the overtime. Of course, all these savings are based on getting an equally productive hour's work on an overtime basis as you do on a regular hourly basis. There is a balance to be struck here. You should add people if you find that you are working your people excessive amounts of overtime for months at a time.

In addition to or in place of the overtime solution, you can add a shift. Adding a shift allows you to take advantage of your existing equipment. Usually the only increase in management expense is for any necessary additional direct supervision for the new shift. However, additional employees will create the added expenses we were saving in our discussion above by working overtime, such as additional insurances and training, etc.

Adding Equipment

There are opportunities to create flexibility by adding equipment or duplicating equipment.

I can't believe the number of times that I have witnessed one operator waiting for another operator to finish with an inexpensive hand tool or power tool so that he or she could use the same tool. This is an area where a skilled engineer can really earn his or her keep by finding the optimum tool and equipment solutions. Better yet, train all your people to look for opportunities like this.

Adding a piece of equipment can eliminate an operator wasting time by moving work to another area, necessitating a change in setup and the waste of material in adjusting for the setup. However, the biggest savings can come not in the set-

130

up time savings or the travel to and from the other area, but in inventory, by eliminating the need to make product in batches. With the equipment right where it is needed, the product can be made as needed because the equipment is always set up and ready to go to work. Also, by adding equipment, an outsourced operation can be eliminated. This can save days of inventory time as well as shipping and handling costs, not to mention the paperwork of moving outsourced material back and forth.

An excellent example of gaining flexibility by combining equipment took place in a company in Connecticut. The idea was to eliminate having to stock hundreds of product variations that customers would request on short notice. The company was distributing x-ray equipment to thousands of customers. The number of possible combinations for a final product including its accessories was well over ten thousand possibilities. The problem was how to provide for same-day delivery of all combinations of product without maintaining huge inventories. The solution was to finish building the product in the Shipping department to each customer's request. The end result was a pack-and-ship-area that did the final assembly of the finished product. Assembly equipment was moved into the shipping area along with all the individual components that together made up the ten thousand possible combinations. Items that created the variations were several types of filters, end covers, heat exchangers, fans, several cable lengths, different mounting devices, collimating devices and finally colors. Even a paint booth and baking station were constructed to over-spray each unit with the custom colors ordered by the customers. The product was shipped the same day the customer's order was received. Combining the final assembly function with the shipping function in one area and relocating the equipment for the final assembly created the flexibility to gain a competitive edge—the ability to deliver to the customer the same day when the competition couldn't.

Similarly, adding automatic cut-off saws to a raw material warehouse created the flexibility needed to eliminate

131

many different sizes of bar stock. This saved thousands of dollars in raw material inventory. Adding the automatic cut-off saws added flexibility by permitting the material to be cut to any size desired.

New ways of thinking for equipment operators are sometimes required when adding new machinery that increases flexibility. Adding a machining center with automatic pallet changers and tool changers to an in-house operation enabled us to bring functions inside our facility that had previously been subcontracted to outside vendors. Flexibility was created by eliminating all the queuing and manufacturing time necessary for the outside vendors to do their portion of the machining. This allowed us to start and finish a product without interruption. This is a tough goal to achieve whenever you find it necessary mid-stream to send the item outside your facility for further processing, then bring it back for further work inside your facility. To get back to the operator: when the operator was first introduced to his new machine, he would shut the equipment down during his coffee breaks. On a visit to this area, seeing the machine idle, I asked the operator if the machine was down for repair. He told me: "Oh no, I am on my coffee break." After I asked him if he thought the machine needed a break too, the light came on. The machine was not privileged to any future coffee breaks from that day on.

A very successful Team using innovative ideas to improve equipment and processes operated as a Cross-Functional Self-Directed Team in one of my businesses. The end result of the Team's efforts was a 30 percent reduction in floor space, a 50 percent reduction in inventory and a direct labor reduction of 1,500 hours a month, which represented more than 25 percent of the total available monthly hours in this area. These people did not lose their jobs as a result of their efforts to reduce labor hours. Excessive overtime had been worked in this area as well as in other areas of this business. As these employees were cross-trained to perform several functions in other areas of the business, they were used to reduce the need for overtime. As a result, the 1,500 hours were absorbed. Working a fair amount of overtime in your business gives you the flexibility to absorb the excess labor that results from this kind of innovation. All you have to do is replace some of the overtime with the excess labor created, provided you have a well cross-trained workforce. These circumstances make it easier to get the full cooperation of your people. They will not be worried about eliminating their own jobs.

Swapping Equipment

Replacing old equipment with automated equipment can pay off big. In one of my businesses I replaced older test equipment that was used to test medical equipment functionality by simulating patient conditions. It was necessary to document the testing by printing and storing the test results in a "device history folder." These folders were one half to one inch thick, filled with test documentation for each monitor. This test equipment was replaced with test equipment that downloaded the product history test results automatically onto a server. This eliminated the thick "device history folders" and all the costs associated with creating, maintaining and storing them.

Improving Equipment

Mistake Proofing your processes will lead to equipment improvements. As discussed previously, Statistical Process Control (SPC), capability studies can identify problems with tooling and/or the calibration of the machines.

Moving Equipment

The simple task of examining the location of equipment within your facility can lead to increased efficiency. By diagramming the flow of product through your facility, you can reveal items that are taking a circuitous route. Combining equipment in one area can eliminate queue time, travel time,

133

and batch building. This can reduce inventory and improve velocity and quality.

If copiers or printers are used in your business process, then get them out of the offices and place them where they are used. Also, if scales are needed, move those scales to the best locations. If water or drains are required, see that they are in the work area. Hand tools and fixtures should be close by. If transactions are done in the work area, have scanners and/or terminals close by. If bar-codes are printed in the process, have bar-code printers nearby. Work area design is so important to your success.

The above are just a few examples; the possibilities are virtually endless. The best way to pursue these issues is to involve your employees. These types of projects are fun and exciting opportunities for your Self-Directed Teams to work on.

Creating Labor Flexibility Through Training

There is a certain amount of labor flexibility inherent in any operation that is not working three full shifts, seven days a week. You can always work overtime, adding to your total available hours. This overtime is not as costly as it first appears, as described above. However, we will not be concentrating on this type of flexibility here. The type of flexibility we will be focusing on here is that flexibility gained from having a well cross-trained workforce. In my businesses it was not unheard of to have an employee doing one job in the morning, another in the afternoon, and an entirely different job the next day. Some of these businesses were Union Shops, so no excuses on that score. Gaining the support of the Union is simply a function of negotiating away many of the unnecessary labor grades and job classifications. This is the type of flexibility you will need, if you are going to maintain excellent velocity with little inventory. And you need to maintain excellent velocity, if you are going to be a world-class organization that satisfies your customer's ever-changing needs. Remember, if you don't satisfy your customer's needs, your competition will. If you have no competitors to worry about today, and you don't satisfy your customer's needs, you will soon have competitors and they will satisfy your customer's needs.

Reward for Skills Learned

One way to encourage your employees to learn new skills is to make it profitable for them. This can be accomplished by basing pay grades or hourly rates on the number of skill sets an employee has accomplished. After all, the more an employee knows, the more valuable he or she is to the organization. Rather than paying a person for the skill level they are currently performing at and locking them into one task or set of skills, you pay them for all the skills they have mastered. This gives you the option to use them wherever their skills are most needed at any given moment, thereby creating greater flexibility for your organization. When you are paying employees for all the skills they have mastered, you and your management team will tend to be more ready to move these workers to the jobs where they are most needed to satisfy current demand. This moves you away from the mode of doing unnecessary busy work, just so you can keep your people (who only know how to perform tasks that have no current demand) occupied. Creating inventory just to keep them busy is counter-productive.

If you truly have no work other than creating inventory that you have no current demand for, send those people to the cafeteria, buy them coffee and give them a deck of cards. If this is a regular problem in your business, then you have too many people. Keeping too many people on the payroll does no one a favor. The amount of work available always has a tendency to expand to consume the number of labor hours available to do the work. If you have thirty-five hours of work and forty hours of labor available, somehow the thirty-five hours of work will take forty hours. The only way to win at this game is to make sure that you always have less labor available than is needed, then work a modest amount of

135

overtime to make up for any shortage of labor. Also, when there are more people than you need in your business, these folks will find a way to amuse themselves. This does not always result in a positive experience for the company or the employee. Look for excess labor problems in areas of your business where employees are frequently bickering.

There are many ways to encourage your employees to learn the various skills they will need in your new "World Class" company. Recognition for mastering new skills or completion of a training program can take several forms, such as job promotions, certificates, luncheons honoring their achievements, announcements, articles in the company or local newspaper, cash awards, etc. These can all be powerful motivators. Talk up training. Make sure your people understand that training is a valuable benefit, an investment the company is making in them personally, which provides a measure of job protection. Communicate that the training enhances their value in the overall job marketplace. Explain that they are responsible for and should take charge of their own career. You can provide the opportunity and encouragement, but they must put forth the effort and energy to execute well.

It is never easy to move work to a Low Cost Country. However, it happens with regularity these days. If you have a highly-trained workforce, they will be in high demand and this will be their best chance to find new work quickly. I moved a business from Connecticut to Bangalore, India. The workforce in Connecticut was highly trained. In addition to the normal job skills they took with them, they were Six Sigma trained and had used Statistical Process Control Lean techniques for years. These workers had received extensive training in Poka-yoke (Mistake Proofing). Our employees were in such high demand that several area employers ran job fairs in our facility in an attempt to convince these highly-trained workers to sign up with them for jobs when our facility finally closed. It wasn't very long after that virtually everyone who wanted a job had one, even in a very tough job market. Many of these folks

136

were able to bank their bonuses and severance pay and return to work right away—knowing this sure helps one sleep better at night.

Flow Manufacturing Makes Training More Important

To react to customer demand, the available labor will have to be able to perform the tasks required to fill the current orders, no matter what they are. Customer orders rarely arrive in the mix that exactly complements the skill sets of your available labor, unless there is enough flexibility built into your labor force to meet almost any possible combination of demands. You may correctly forecast monthly sales of four hundred of product "A" and four hundred of product "B," but the orders may arrive for two hundred of product "A" during the first and last week of the month and two hundred of product "B" during the second and third week of the month. If only half your labor force had the skills necessary to fill orders for product "A" and the other half had only the skills necessary fill orders for "B," then during the first and fourth weeks of the month when you only had orders for product "A," the half of the workforce that had only the skills necessary to fill orders for product "B" would be idle. During the second and third weeks of the month, the workers who had only the skills to fill orders for product "A" would be idle. Furthermore, assuming you had enough total labor available to fill only eight hundred total units during the month, you would not have the necessary available product to satisfy either customer in a timely manner because half your labor force would be idle during the entire month. This is a very simple scenario. Of course, in real life there are usually many more than two products, and the orders arrive even more erratically than illustrated in this scenario, making the necessity for labor flexibility even more important.

In several of my businesses, adding various well-trained management and staff employees to the available

137

direct labor pool during peak demand periods enhanced flexibility. Everybody seemed to enjoy the change of pace brought about by an opportunity to actually help fill orders for product. The Managers and Supervisors got some good hands-on experience, which often led to positive changes in methods, or at least to a better appreciation of the direct labor activities. The direct labor folks got a chance to harass the management in a friendly and playful way. The pizza was always on the company and the drinks were always soft and plentiful. On many occasions, employees were encouraged to take dinner home from the company. This appeased the spouses, who were either home waiting for their dinner or relieved that they didn't have to cook dinner when their spouse arrived home late from work. Again, this was done in a Union Shop. Remember, for twenty-two years I operated in a Union environment in different companies. I always had a deal with the Union that went like this: as long as I was offering unlimited overtime to all employees, non-union employees were allowed to pitch in. If your Union is stricter, there is usually a deal you can work out, provided you have excellent relations with your Union. Excellent relations with your Union start with a mutual respect and will be only as good as the relations you have with your employees.

Simple Matrix

A simple matrix can be used to manage skill levels for your employees. Each Manager should create and maintain a matrix with the names of the employees they are responsible for down the left side of the page and the different job functions or skill sets performed in their area across the top. An X is placed across from the employee's name and under the skill set that the employee has mastered. The Manager's job is to encourage each employee to master as many skills as practically possible. Post the matrix in a very visible place for all to see. There is nothing like creating a little peer pressure and competition to get the ball rolling. The matrix must be well maintained or it will lose its effectiveness. Jobs in other areas not directly included in the manager's area of responsibility should be included on the matrix. This will enable managers to draw from other pools of trained labor when they have high labor demands and vice versa. All direct Supervisors should work on completing the matrixes together to ensure cross-fertilization. Goals can be established, such as: all employees should know how to do at least three distinct jobs by the end of the year. Each Supervisor should also be evaluated and rewarded, based on how well he or she does at cross-training employees.

Full-Time Trainer

If your organization can afford it, a full-time trainer can prove to be a very valuable addition to your facility. I don't see how you cannot afford to add a full-time trainer if you have more than one hundred employees. In today's business environment, with all the required EHS (Environmental Health and Safety) training, as well as training required by other governmental organizations, a full-time trainer on-site is almost a must-have, and he or she will certainly pay their own way many times over. The training is going to be done one way or the other, so why not have a professional maximize on the opportunity? In addition to the EHS training, the trainer can cover new employee orientation, HR training such as harassment training, management development, ISO training, Mistake Proofing, computer skills, as well as basic job skills. In addition, your trainer can maintain the necessary compliance records of the training that are required by so many governmental and quasi-governmental organizations.

My trainers have been involved in all of the above training efforts. They became trusted members of our Team, keeping records of the skills each employee mastered and scheduling employees for regular refresher courses. If they had a course with only three employees scheduled to attend, and there was room for eight in the class, they would post a notice on the classroom door offering the course to any volunteer who wanted to learn the skill they were teaching. We encouraged any employee who wanted to take the course to do so on our time. The classes were usually full. The trainer can also pitch in during peak periods when an extra pair of hands is needed in any of the many areas he or she has expertise in.

It was important for our employees to understand what great assets they possessed in the skills they had developed over the years they had served their company. They were valuable and valued employees. Understanding this value would drive them to learn even more to further ensure that they would always be marketable employees. Our philosophy was, "Why would we want an employee on our payroll that nobody else wanted?" Sure, we lost some of our best to other area employers, but very few left us. Our turnover rate was less than two percent annually and some of the two percent was due to retirement.

Chapter 8

Chapter 8

Succession Planning

In today's fast-moving business environment Succession Planning is no longer a luxury; no longer is it something you can keep putting off or keep promising yourself you will get around to in the near future. It is essential NOW! Today, if you don't keep improving your employees' skills and talents on an ongoing basis, they will become outdated and you will have to fire all your people and hire new ones every five years or so to remain competitive. The world is moving that fast. Also, employees are very mobile and always looking for better opportunities. Unfortunately, you usually lose the best employees to the competition—no one wants your worst employees. When you stop and think about it, would you want an employee nobody else wants? So how do you protect your business? The answer is a solid Succession Plan. Create as deep a bench as your business can afford.

You will derive many benefits from a good executable plan. As you prepare your employees to replace someone on the next level up, you will be developing their skills. Once they are tagged for advancement, an investment in preparing them for their new role will be called for.

A proper plan must be formal. It should be well documented and reviewed at least monthly. It is okay to create a new plan once a year that takes into consideration changes in the business and in the competitive climate, as well as considerations of how well the chosen candidates are progressing. However, the plan must be reviewed regularly throughout the year to be effective.

The initial plan should encompass all key employees in the business. Starting with the Business Leader, he or she should identify an individual who is prepared to take his or her place immediately. If a candidate is not immediately available, a weakness in the organization has been identified. At this point, preparation to groom a replacement should begin in earnest. There is always the possibility that there is no worthy candidate currently available in the business. Under these circumstances, the organization will have to look to the outside for a replacement. Barring unusual circumstances, this is a failure of leadership to execute one of their most important responsibilities—to perpetuate the business. Perpetuating the business not only means paying taxes, obeying the laws, securing the proper permits and licenses, etc. It also means doing the things that ensure that the business will survive and thrive in the future.

After the Leader's replacement has been identified, it is prudent to tag another candidate to be prepped for the position. This is in case the first candidate should not work out. The first candidate may be the perfect candidate; however, he or she may leave the company for some reason. In this case, you would not want to start grooming a replacement from scratch. Depending on how close you are to needing a replacement, the potential replacements need not know they are the chosen ones. If they were aware of their status and for some reason you were forced to select another individual to take the leadership role, there would be a good chance of losing a good employee to the competition.

How many candidates you have lined up to fill a particular role will depend on the importance of that role and on the size of the organization. You do not have to have a second successor for every key role in your organization. If a key role is very similar to several other key roles in your business, you may tag an individual to fill more than one slot. This assumes that it is unlikely that you would lose several individuals in the same role all at the same time. Be reasonable; don't tag one person to fill ten slots at the same time. Again, it is not necessary to tag ten individuals to replace ten other individuals who are doing the same or very similar jobs.

After you have addressed the succession plan for the Business Leader, move on and do the same thing for each member of the Leadership Team. Then continue on through the organization until you have addressed each and every key role in your business. The plan should be built by the individual currently filling the role being addressed. Each individual's succession plan should be reviewed at least one level up on a regular basis throughout the year.

The plan should include:

- The name of the current planned successor.
- Readiness status—how ready is the individual to take over the role.
- The target date by which the successor will be fully prepared for the responsibility.
- What steps are necessary to prepare the individual for the responsibility—this should be a detailed plan with action steps and commitment dates.
- The backup candidate identified should the current planned successor drop out.
- Approval at least one level up.

Each planner should be measured as to the effectiveness of their plan. It should be a part of their annual performance review. Part of the potential salary adjustment should be a direct result of the Succession Planning effectiveness. Again, there are two main goals of a Succession Planning program—employee development and preparing employees to take over for people we lose. Both are equally important.

CHAPTER 9

CHAPTER 9

Expense Control

Who Should Own the Cost Accounting Function

Okay, let's start out with a rather controversial concept. At least, most accountants will think it is a controversial concept at first glance. However, on closer examination they should love the concept. Here it is: place responsibility for Cost Accounting and all related functions with the Operations departments. What better way to control costs than to make the Operations Leaders the ones responsible for measuring and analyzing their own costs? After all, real control of labor, material and equipment costs rests with the operating folks, not with the accountants. Responsibility, accountability and authority go together; you can't have one without the other two. I am not suggesting that Finance give up all controllership and oversight for operating costs. I am in favor of strong controllership, but cooperative controllership with the acknowledgment that the main purpose is to assist the folks who create the value in the business—namely, the Operations folks—whether the business is construction, manufacturing, distribution, or service-related. I am suggesting that those folks responsible for Cost Accounting functions, or whatever

149

your organization calls them, report solid line to the operating organization and dotted line to the Finance organization. I have successfully used this form of reporting for years. It has brought great understanding to the operating groups, leading to good solid cost management in the businesses involved.

Monitoring Labor Costs

So in our new organization, how are we going to monitor labor costs without work orders? Easy—we use the time and attendance records to collect total labor hours for an area. This could be a product line, a construction project, a group of services, or any activity that involves direct labor. Compare the total number of actual hours collected to the standard hours for the output—the products or services produced and delivered. The difference is over-absorbed or under-absorbed labor hours. In other words: if John and Jim worked a total of eighty hours to deliver twenty widgets, each widget represents four actual labor hours. If the standard for the widget is five hours, labor is over-absorbed by one hour for each widget delivered or a total over-absorption of twenty hours. If both John and Jim make $10 an hour, the labor is over-absorbed by a total of $200.

Of course, for the above to work you have to know what the standard time required to deliver a widget is. Your operating folks can periodically monitor their processes to determine a fair standard. Allowances can be made for setup, breaks and personal time, etc. Analysis of actual trends will tell you when it is time to revisit the standard. More importantly, chronic and persistent occurrences of under-absorbed labor may be an indication of a process problem, material problems, equipment problems, or other as yet undetected problems. These red flags should be investigated to root out and correct the process problems.

Using the Data

You should be using this data to ferret out problems with your processes. This data should not be used to persecute your workers. If you are having a problem with absorption and you cannot find a process problem, talk to your people.

Controlling Other Costs—Where to Look for Cost Savings

Labor Hours

Overtime reduction is a good place to look for possible reduction. However, it also can be very profitable to work overtime. As discussed above, provided you are getting a good hour's work during the overtime hours, it may actually cost you less to work overtime in some businesses. The overtime pay can cost less than hiring another full-time employee when you consider the added costs to carry a new employee on your payroll. If you find that you are working too many overtime hours and that this is causing either poor productivity or a truly higher hourly cost, add more workers to your work force. As pointed out earlier, if you are working a lot of overtime, it is always easier to get the cooperation of your direct labor employees when you start a process improvement program that will end up reducing labor hours. Initially, no one will lose their job and it may give you the time you need to make reductions in force through attrition rather than layoffs.

In addition, use your standard cost system to determine whether overtime has become a habit. If you have a good cost system in place, it should be easy to detect a lower output rate per hour. Of course, the opposite is true: the same or higher output per hour gives assurance that overtime is required. The proper use of overtime is necessary to create the flexibility for labor we need in operating our continuous improvement

151

programs. It is important that it be managed carefully and not abused.

Temporary workers and contractors have their place in a flexible business. They can help reduce the number of required overtime hours. Temps and contractors can be less costly than adding regular employees because they usually do not enjoy the same expensive benefits that regular workers do. The same goes for part-timers; they usually don't share in benefit programs to the same extent as regular employees, making them cost less. But don't forget to constantly reassess their need. Also, remember that it is easier and less costly to layoff this type of employee. They understand that their position with the company is not permanent.

It may be possible to eliminate an entire shift. If you are working two or three shifts and can cut one out completely, you will save the overhead costs associated with running another shift. Some of these costs are shift supervision, heat and air-conditioning, additional security and additional maintenance.

Process improvements to remove labor provide excellent opportunities for cost reductions. Eliminating rework and improving yield is high on this list. Work simplification usually results in labor cost savings. Also, outsourcing items that can be contracted to an outside vendor for a lower cost is a great way to save, provided it would not affect your throughput, velocity, or customer satisfaction. Any item that does not fit your core competency should be *considered* for outsourcing.

Equipment Leases

Review all equipment leases for opportunity. Look at copiers, shipping dock equipment, trucks, cars and storage trailers. A better deal may be available now for your current or expiring leases. The equipment being leased may no longer be necessary; if this is so, return it. This is especially true with storage trailers; once on your property, they tend to be used, needed or not. If the material stored in these trailers is obsolete, get rid of it and return the trailers. The same applies to offsite storage facility leases. The key to controlling these costs is a constant review and justification for keeping the lease open. It may be less costly at some point to buy out a lease than to continue leasing. Leases have a tendency to become evergreen; they just go on and on forever, earning the green for the leaser.

Services

Review items like IT services, carpets, alarm systems, fire extinguishers, sprinkler system servicing and phone-related services like music to make sure you are getting the most for your dollar. Equipment servicing for things like fork trucks, bailers, dock lifters and other machinery should be reviewed regularly. Assign someone to watch over these expenses and review them on a regular basis. Almost every company of significant size has some sort of service expense they are paying for that either is no longer needed or can be replaced with an alternate, less expensive method. These are expenses that get forgotten in the busy day-to-day running of a business.

Defect Costs

Eliminating defect costs is essential. In the 1960s a company could survive with even a 10 percent defect rate. However, in the 1970s defect rates fell below 10 percent and in the early 1980s and 1990s world competition demanded defect rates of less than 1 percent. Today the target has to be zero defects and it is not uncommon to hear of defects being measured in parts per million, as with Six Sigma quality levels, which are 3.4 DPMO (defects per million opportunities). It is obvious that a company with a 5 percent defect rate today is in serious trouble, and there are many businesses with defect rates for products and services at these levels in some areas.

In addition to the labor, material and overhead cost that went into the item or service, defects can reduce your top line through lost revenue. High internal defect rates usually also show up with your customers. These are the worst failures because your customers find them for you. If a customer buys only one product or service from you and that product or service is defective, everything he has ever bought from you is no good. He will be reluctant to try your product or service again.

Increased warranty costs are usually directly related to a high rate of product failure. When you are generating a high failure rate, your process is out of control. As a consequence, your business can be compromised or even lost to the competition.

Many rules have their exceptions. One business I was connected with sold a warranty that assured a customer that he would be supplied with a sensor for a period of time, one year for one price, two years for another higher price and three years for a still higher price. As an example, let's say the item with a thirty-day warranty was sold for around $100. The item with a one-year warranty was sold for $1,000. The item cost $18 to make. The warranty was for a no-questions-asked replacement, as many as needed during the year. If the customer did not use any replacements in the year, he would receive a $300 credit toward the next year's extension, which cost another $1,000. If not for the fact that these sensors experienced common failures, it would not have been possible to sell these warranty plans. A few things to remember: first, the product quality was on par with the competition; second, these circumstances are very rare. Unless you find yourself in a similar situation, you had better eliminate your product or service quality issues. Warranty expenses and business success or failure are closely related.

Supplies

There are two sides to reducing these expenses. Get the best price you can for items like protective gear, but remember the purpose is to protect employees. Don't skimp on small tools. Consider the situation described earlier, where employees waited for another employee to finish with a small hand tool so they could use the same tool because there was only one in the area. Recall, too, the situation where employees had to spend fifteen minutes looking for a flash light to locate items in a poorly lit warehouse. This kind of nonsense is pure waste but is still seen all too often.

Utilities

Phones—good shopping for the correct plan and equipment usually pays off. Here the scene is changing all the time. Stay on top of the changes and offerings, but don't disrupt your business to save a few pennies. Cell phones and smartphones are prolific. They can be great tools; however, these items can become a status symbol rather than a business tool. Everyone will want one for the status that goes with the device. Guard against this by really justifying their need before handing them out. One way to administer these items is to let the employee sign up for a personal plan in their own name and then pay for a portion of the plan for allowing company calls.

Electricity, water and gas also provide opportunities for cost savings. In one operation I was with, energy was over 7 percent of the total product cost. A third shift was added for high power testing, primarily to take advantage of the lower electric rates in the late evening and early morning hours. Boilers that can run on both gas and oil can produce savings by using the fuel that is the cheapest when you are buying and switching back and forth between fuels when necessary.

Depreciation

Unneeded assets that can be transferred or sold should be. If not, they will continue to take up valuable floor space and may even require maintenance or periodic calibration. If the unused equipment is considered to be in service, it will be on the preventative maintenance schedule, which means it will receive periodic scheduled maintenance. The same is true for equipment needing calibration; it will be sucking up technical resources to calibrate a piece of equipment no longer needed. Also, your depreciation list should be reviewed to ferret out non-existent assets that have been disposed of but not removed from the asset list. Do these things routinely to reduce your depreciation expense.

Freight

This area is usually loaded with low-hanging fruit. Look for vendors with several freight charges on the same day. Charging freight for multiple deliveries when several items arrived in the same package is a common error suppliers make. Do not pay for freight on items hand-carried to your business by suppliers. Buyers should try to get the supplier to pay for delivery. When you do pay for freight, make sure you agreed to pay this charge. When you ship, make sure you ship for the lowest cost for the required service. Sensitize your own folks to the abuses of shipping overnight when it is not really necessary. These are only a few suggestions to get the ball rolling. As you take smaller and smaller deliveries more frequently, freight charges will take on more significance and require better management.

Calibration

As mentioned above, equipment not in service should be formally removed from service to prevent unnecessary calibration. This can require one last calibration to prove that the last items calibrated using this equipment were being calibrated to build specification. Analyze your calibration costs to determine whether it is better to do your own calibration or employ an outside service.

Other Areas to Explore for Cost Savings that May Be Overlooked Are:

- Housekeeping costs, including the cost of space used to store obsolete items.

- Dispose of obsolete items early to produce the biggest return on the sale. Age will rarely enhance the value of obsolete items.

- Product packaging costs can yield nice savings. Be on the lookout for revolutionary packaging methods. Some of the newer packaging methods are environmentally friendly as well as cost effective.

- Travel and entertainment costs can be reviewed for reductions. Be careful here; do not forget to celebrate successes—even small ones.

- Discretionary meetings can be cut altogether or held "in company" rather than at a local hotel.

- Identify space you pay for and maybe don't use. Isolate it, close it off, and turn off the lights and air conditioning, or even relocate to a smaller location.

- Assign expenses that are allocated over several areas of responsibility to an owner. If nobody feels responsible for these expenses, the likelihood of their being optimized is slim.

- Review decisions to make or purchase items such as CDs and manuals. Changes in technology may make it profitable to perform certain tasks in-house that you are

157

currently outsourcing. One example is the CD that is shipped as documentation with your product. Current technology makes it not only cost effective to make in-house or delivered over the net; it can also be a logistics as well as an inventory advantage, especially when many different versions of the software are required.

Although many of the costs discussed here are not necessarily part of the direct product cost, they can still have a significant impact on overall costs. A key to controlling these costs is not to lose sight of them. Assign one primary owner and add to this list your own set of costs that need controlling and review them on a regular basis.

EPILOGUE: A FINAL WORD

Don't just put this book down and go back to doing business as usual.

- *Take a look at your business.*
- *Compare your own business processes to the ones described in this book.*
- *Get your employees involved in converting your business into a Lean money-making enterprise.*

Actions say more than words and your words must be backed by actions. Your company can achieve similar or even greater results. Your employees can do it for you. Just ask them, they are ready to help.

159

Sources

Buckley, Ronald L., Winning in a Highly Competitive Manufacturing Environment, Shady Brook Press, 2003

Buckley, Ronald L. and Buckley, Candace-Lynn, No Eraser Needed: Mistake Proofing Your Business, Sax Macy Fromm, 2012

Buckley, Ronald L. and Buckley, Lucinda A., My Toaster's Grandfather, Shady Brook Press, 2012

Buckley, Ronald L. and Buckley, Lucinda A., Winning Manufacturing Solutions, Shady Brook Press, 2012

Drucker, Peter F., The Effective Executive, Butterworth-Heinemann, 2004.

Galsworth, Gwendolyn D., The Visual Systems: Harnessing the Power of a Visual Workplace, AMACOM, American Management Association, 1997.

Katzenbach, Jon R. and Smith, Douglas K., The Wisdom of Teams: Creating the High-Performance Organization, Harper Business—Division of Harper Collins Publishers, New York, New York, 1994.

Pande, Peter S., Neuman, Robert P. and Cavanagh, Roland R., The Six Sigma Way, McGraw-Hill Company, New York, New York, 2000.

Schonberger, Richard J., World Class Manufacturing: The Next Decade, Building Power, Strength, and Value, The Free Press, 1996.

Shigeo Shingo, Zero Quality Control: Source Inspection and the Poka-yoke System, Productivity Press, Stamford, CT and Cambridge, MA, 1986.

Wiig, John H., Fix That Business, John Wiig, 2012

165

Made in the USA
San Bernardino, CA
20 January 2016